# Sage Financial Controller

# Training Guide

Incorporating:

Bookkeeper
Accountant
Accountant+
Financial Controller

**Dexter J Booth**

Pitman

PITMAN PUBLISHING
128 Long Acre, London, WC2E 9AN

A Division of Longman Group UK Limited

© Dexter J Booth 1992

First published in Great Britain 1992

British Library Cataloguing-in-Publication Data

A catalogue record for this book is available from the British Library.

ISBN 0 273 03763 3

Printed and bound in Great Britain.

# Contents

## Section D: Ending the month's accounting 76

## Section E: The second month 104

# Introduction

The Sage Sterling Accounting system is available in each of four components:

**Bookkeeper**
**Accountant**
**Accountant +**
**Financial Controller**

The Financial Controller component permits full use of all facilities offered by the system whereas Bookkeeper offers restricted facilities. This *Guide* caters for each component by ensuring that whichever is available to you, the facilities that it offers are considered in detail.

Imagine that you are living on a remote Hebridean island and making a living by buying oysters and salmon and selling them to a variety of customers on the mainland. In addition, you buy firewood from the mainland and sell it to various people on the island. For some time your business has been developing, from small beginnings, but now you find that the market for your wares has increased sufficiently to warrant a capital injection from your private funds and a bank loan enabling you to expand the enterprise.

As you work through this *Guide* you will see the company develop and at the same time learn how the Sage Sterling Accounting system can be used to keep a track of your affairs.

# Getting Started ▬▬▬▬▬▬▬▬▬

**Installation**

The Sage Sterling Accounting Software arrives at your door on a collection of floppy diskettes accompanied by a set of three manuals; the System Manager, the Installation guide and the Accounting manual. In the first instance the most important of these is the Installation manual for it is in there that explicit instructions are given that permit you to install the Sage Sterling Accounting system onto your computer.

In this Training Guide it is assumed that the Sage Sterling Accounting system has been installed onto a hard disk (drive C) into a sub-directory called SAGE. To activate the system from the DOS prompt:

**C:\\>**

displayed on your computer screen, enter the following instruction to change directory to the SAGE sub-directory:

**cd SAGE**

followed by **RETURN**. The prompt will now look as follows:

**C:\\SAGE>**

Now type in the command:

**SAGE**

followed by **RETURN** and the Sage Sterling Accounting system will become activated.

When you first run the system you will be asked to enter your company name and address. There is one line for the name and four for the address. Each line must contain at least 8 characters but not more than 25 and the only punctuation that is permitted is a full stop. Once entered, your company name and address will be printed at the head of every report you produce so make sure that you *do not make a mistake*. If you do make a mistake then press the **ESC** key and start again.

For the purposes of this *Guide* I shall be using the following company name and address:

**Erin Fish Supplies**
**Barchantrum**
**Kinloch**
**Isle of Erin**
**EO1 1OE**

If you are learning how to use this package with a view to using it for your own personal business affairs then I would suggest that you use the same company name and default date that I do so that all your work will be consistent with the text of the *Guide*. When you have worked through the *Guide* and feel happy enough to take off on your own then reinstall the system onto the hard disk from your master floppy diskettes and set up your own personal accounts.

If you are a college student learning how to use this package from a networked PC then, in all probability, you will not be able to store your data files on the hard disk. In this case you will need a formatted floppy diskette resident in the external drive that has been initialised by the Sage Sterling Accounting system. Furthermore, you will not be able to change the company name to the one I have suggested. This is of little matter and you should proceed with whatever company name has been given on the college network.

Having entered your company name you will be asked to enter the date and a default date will be displayed. For the purposes of this Training Guide the date we shall be using to begin with is 1 August 1992. Type this date into the space alloted on the screen in the form:

**010892**

Now press **RETURN** after which you will be asked for a password. The password is:

**LETMEIN**

Type this in and you will notice an X appear in response to each character typed. Not displaying your password as it is entered helps to maintain its security. When you have typed in the password press **RETURN** and the Sage Sterling Main Menu will appear - your entry point into the entire accounting package.

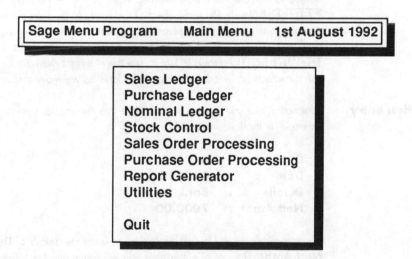

```
Sage Menu Program    Main Menu    1st August 1992
```

```
Sales Ledger
Purchase Ledger
Nominal Ledger
Stock Control
Sales Order Processing
Purchase Order Processing
Report Generator
Utilities

Quit
```

This screen may not be exactly what you see, depending upon which category of package you are using. The Financial Controller, however, encompasses all facilities available within the system and so that is what is reproduced above.

**Function keys**

Having entered the Sage Sterling Accounting system and having arrived at the Main Menu we should take note of the various facilities offered by the function keys labelled **F1** and **F2**.

The Function key **F1** provides Help on the particular screen displayed. With the Main Menu on display press **F1** and the following display appears.

> **To select an option from the menu :-**
>
> **Move the cursor using the [ARROW] keys until it is positioned over the relevant option and press the RETURN key.**
>
> **or**
>
> **Press the first letter of the relevant menu option and press the RETURN key**
>
> **Press [ESC] to return to a previous menu.**

To remove the Help display press the **ESC** key. Now press the **F2** function key and a calculator appears in the top left hand corner of the screen. You can use this calculator during the execution of the package and we shall see how to do this later. For now it is sufficient that we know it is available. Press the **ESC** key and the calculator disappears.

### Cursor Control keys

Finally, we need to know how to use the various cursor control keys available on the keyboard. These are the **UP**, **DOWN**, **LEFT** and **RIGHT** arrow keys and the **BACK SPACE** key. During the operation of the system you will occasionally see a list of words or phrases as you now do in the Main Menu. One of these words or phrases will be highlighted to indicate that the highlighted word or phrase is ready to be activated by pressing **RETURN**. We shall see the effect of this later. At the moment we must consider the situation where the word or phrase highlighted is not the one we desire to be activated. In such a case we move the highlight with the cursor control keys. Try it now. Press the **DOWN** and **UP** arrows in turn to see the highlight move up and down the list. We shall see the effects of the other cursor control keys as we move through the *Guide*.

### Information entry

Information that you are required to enter into the various screens is given in tables. For example, in the following table:

**Dept** : **0**
**Date** : **010892**
**Details** : **Bank loan**
**Nett Amnt** : **7000.00**

the screen display will be asking for you to enter the details of **Dept**, **Date**, **Details** and **Nett Amnt**. The actual entries that you will make into the screen, via the keyboard, against these items are listed to the right of the colons which are there merely to separate the screen item heading from the actual entry.

# Section A: Setting up the system ▬▬▬▬

You are a sole trader located on the Isle of Erin in the Hebrides. Your company, Erin Fish Supplies, has been trading for some time now but on a small, part-time scale. Recently you have discovered a growing market for your wares and you have decided to expand. This increased business means that you have less time available for writing your accounts by hand so you have decided to invest in a small personal computer and the Sage Sterling Accounting system.

In this Section you will learn how to set up your accounting system in readiness for entering the transactions resulting from your future continuous trading.

The following table describes which of the Tasks in this Section are available in which component of the Sage Sterling Accounting system:

| Task | 1 | 2 | 3 | 4 | 5 | 6 | 7 | 8 | 9 | 10 | 11 | 12 | 13 | 14 |
|---|---|---|---|---|---|---|---|---|---|---|---|---|---|---|
| Bookkeeper | yes | yes | yes | yes | yes | yes | yes | yes* | yes | yes | yes | no | no | no |
| Accountant | yes | yes | yes | yes | yes | yes | yes | yes | yes | yes | yes | yes | yes | yes |
| Accountant + | yes | yes | yes | yes | yes | yes | yes | yes | yes | yes | yes | yes | yes | yes |
| Financial Controller | yes | yes | yes | yes | yes | yes | yes | yes | yes | yes | yes | yes | yes | yes |

*It is not possible to issue a remittance advice from within Bookkeeper

# Reviewing the ledger system

**Objective**

To appreciate the central role played by the Nominal Ledger.

**Instructions**

Enter the system and display the Main Menu.

> **Sales Ledger**
> **Purchase Ledger**
> **Nominal Ledger**
> **Stock Control**
> **Sales Order Processing**
> **Purchase Order Processing**
> **Report Generator**
> **Utilities**
>
> **Quit**

The first three facilities offered by the Main Menu are the three principal ledgers within the accounting system; the Sales, Purchase and Nominal Ledgers.

Every company performs transactions with money and the purpose of the accounting system is to keep a record of both the transactions and the money associated with each transaction. This is done by assigning each transaction to an Account and there are as many different Accounts as there are different types of transaction. If the company buys a van to enable it to deliver its goods there may be a Purchase Account in the name of the company that sold the van and in that Account will be recorded the amount paid for the van - in the jargon of accounting it is said that the purchase invoice for the van will be posted to the Purchase Ledger. If the company sells a quantity of stock to a customer there will be a Sales Account in the name of the customer and all sales invoices to that customer will be posted to that Account. If the company is registered for Value Added Tax (VAT) there will be a Tax Account in which all sales and purchases that involve tax will be posted thereby recording all tax collected and all tax expenditure. The life history of every Account is recorded in a Ledger and to create order amongst the large variety of different Accounts they are grouped into types. Because the principle aim of any company is to buy and sell the two main ledgers are the Sales Ledger and the Purchase Ledger.

**Sales Ledger**

All sales are recorded in the Sales Ledger which contains a collection of Sales Accounts and the amounts of money each account owes the company.

**Purchase Ledger**

All purchases are recorded in the Purchase Ledger which contains a collection of Purchase Accounts and the amounts of money each account is owed by the company.

**Nominal Ledger**

The Nominal Ledger records *every* transaction that the company makes. Every sale recorded in the Sales Ledger is also recorded in the Nominal Ledger as is every purchase. Many Accounts involve transactions that are neither sales nor purchases. For example, Bank Account transactions involve the payment in and the withdrawal out of money. Such transactions may be caused by a sale or a purchase but the transaction itself is neither a sale nor a purchase. This type of transaction is also recorded in the Nominal Ledger. As a consequence the Nominal Ledger contains the complete transaction life history of the company and as such plays a central role in the company's accounting system.

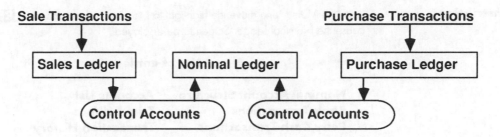

Because the Nominal Ledger stands between the Debtors in the Sales Ledger and the Creditors in the Purchase Ledger it has to keep a balance between the two. This is achieved by a system known as 'double entry' book-keeping. In the ledgers, every recorded Debit in one account is balanced by a Credit of an equal amount in another account and vice versa. As a consequence posting transactions to the Nominal Ledger has to be performed with great care to ensure that the balance is maintained. Fortunately, within the Sage Sterling Accounting System Sales and Purchase transactions that are posted into the Sales and Purchase Ledgers are automatically posted into the Nominal Ledger via the various Control Accounts - we shall see later what these various Control Accounts are. What we now need to consider are the facilities offered by the Nominal Ledger and this we do next.

| Key words | **Transaction** |
| --- | --- |
| | **Account** |
| | **Posting a transaction** |
| | **Sales Ledger** |
| | **Purchase Ledger** |
| | **Nominal Ledger** |
| | **Control Account** |

Task 2                    **Viewing the Nominal Ledger screen**

**Objective**             To view the facilities offered by the Nominal Ledger.

**Instructions**          From the Main Menu move the highlight to Nominal Ledger and press **RETURN**. This will cause the Nominal Ledger Screen to be displayed.

**No. of entries : 0**

| | |
|---|---|
| **Nominal Account Structure** | **Accounts List** |
| **Bank Transactions** | **Trial Balance** |
| **Petty Cash Transactions** | **Transaction History** |
| **Journal Entries** | **Control Account history** |
| **Recurring Entries** | **Day Books** |
| **Prepayments and Accruals** | **VAT Return Analysis** |
| **Depreciation** | **Monthly Accounts** |
| **Quick Ratio** | **Asset Valuation** |

This screen is typical of all such screens within the system. There is a heading to tell you which screen you are looking at. Just below the heading on this screen is the legend:

**No. of entries : 0**

This is telling you that there are no entries in the Nominal Ledger. As we progress through the *Guide* you will see this number increase as entries are made into the ledger.

Below the legend is a list of facilities offered by the Nominal Ledger, some of which relate to posting transactions to the ledger and others which relate to information that can be obtained from the ledger in the form of standard reports. For example, the option Bank Transactions will permit bank deposits and withdrawals to be posted to the Nominal Ledger whereas Trial Balance will produce a report which displays the balanced state of the ledger. To begin our excursion into the ledger we shall consider next the structure of the accounts that it contains.

---

**Key words**            **Nominal Ledger screen**
                         **Posting transactions**
                         **Standard reports**

---

# Viewing the Nominal Ledger Accounts structure

**Objective**

To become aware of the account codes used by the Nominal Ledger.

**Instructions**

From the Nominal Ledger screen press **RIGHT ARROW** to place the highlight over Accounts List and press **RETURN** . This will cause the Accounts List screen to be displayed.

---

**Activity 3.1**

View the Nominal Ledger Account Codes

The legend:

**Lower Account Reference    000000 :**

appears with a flashing cursor in a box to the right. It is possible to enter an account number here but instead we shall accept the default account number of zero and just press **RETURN** .

Now you are asked to enter the Upper Account Reference with default 999999. Again, accept the default by pressing **RETURN** again.

Finally, you are asked whether you want the Accounts List displayed on the screen D, sent to the printer P or sent to a disk file F. The default is D so accept that by pressing **RETURN** and after a few moments the screen fills with the Account Codes under the heading **Ref.** and **Account Name**.

| Ref. | Account Name | Ref. | Account Name |
|------|--------------|------|--------------|
| 0010 | FREEHOLD PROPERTY | 0011 | LEASEHOLD PROPERTY |
| 0020 | PLANT AND MACHINERY | 0021 | P/M DEPRECIATION |
| 0030 | OFFICE EQUIPMENT | 0031 | O/E DEPRECIATION |
| 0040 | FURNITURE AND FIXTURES | 0041 | F/F DEPRECIATION |
| 0050 | MOTOR VEHICLES | 0051 | M/V DEPRECIATION |
| 1001 | STOCK | 1002 | WORK IN PROGRESS |
| 1003 | FINISHED GOODS | 1100 | DEBTORS CONTROL ACCOUNT |
| 1101 | SUNDRY DEBTORS | 1102 | OTHER DEBTORS |
| 1103 | PREPAYMENTS | 1200 | BANK CURRENT ACCOUNT |
| 1210 | BANK DEPOSIT ACCOUNT | 1220 | BUILDING SOCIETY ACCOUNT |
| 1230 | PETTY CASH | 2100 | CREDITORS CONTROL ACCOUNT |
| 2101 | SUNDRY CREDITORS | 2102 | OTHER CREDITORS |
| 2109 | ACCRUALS | 2200 | TAX CONTROL ACCOUNT |
| 2201 | VAT LIABILITY | 2210 | P.A.Y.E. |
| 2211 | NATIONAL INSURANCE | 2230 | PENSION FUND |

At the head of the list on the left hand side is:

**0010 FREEHOLD PROPERTY**

This is telling you that any transaction involving freehold property must be posted using the Nominal Ledger Account Code 0010.

At the bottom of the list is the instruction:

**Press ESC to finish, RETURN to continue**

This, again, is typical of these screen displays. If you press **RETURN** then the screen display will change to reveal the next list of 30 account codes and names. Try it.

When you have read the new display you will see that the instruction at the bottom of the screen is still there. If you were to press **ESC** you would exit the Accounts List and return to the previous screen which was the Nominal Ledger screen. Try it. The **ESC** key is used throughout the system to finish with the current screen and return you to the previous screen.

By returning to the Nominal Ledger screen you have not seen the full extent of the Account structure so repeat this Activity and view all the Accounts. Make sure that when you have viewed all the Accounts and their codes you are back at the Nominal Ledger screen.

---

**Activity 3.2**

Produce a printed copy of the Account Codes

From the Nominal Ledger screen re-select Accounts List and when you are asked:

**Display, Printer or File**

Enter **P** and press **RETURN**. At the prompt:

**Switch the Printer On and Press RETURN**

check that your printer is switched on and On-Line and press **RETURN** again. The entire Accounts List will then be sent to the printer giving you a hard copy that you can peruse at leisure.

It will be worth your while to spend a few moments to read through all the available Account names just to see what is there.

---

**Key words**

**Accounts List**
**Account Names**
**Account Codes**
**ESC** **key**

# Amending the Nominal Accounts structure

**Objective**

To learn how to create Nominal Ledger account names and codes and how to amend existing account names.

**Instructions**

The Account List that you have just viewed is the default list provided by Sage. Because the list may not be appropriate to your existing company account structure the list can be amended to suit your needs. For our purposes we shall accept it as it is with the exception of noting that it has no Account dealing with the startup capital required to start the company. We shall rectify this by creating such an Account. Notice first Accounts 3100 and 3101 named RESERVES and UNDISTRIBUTED RESERVES. We shall create Account 3102 and name it STARTUP CAPITAL.

From the Nominal Ledger Screen select Nominal Account Structure resulting in the Nominal Accounts screen.

> **Account Names**
> **Profit & Loss Format**
> **Balance Sheet Format**

---

**Activity 4.1**

Add an Account

Select Account Names to reveal the Nominal Account Structure screen with a flashing cursor alongside Account Reference. Into this screen enter the number **3102** to give the following display (but do not press **RETURN** just yet):

> **Account Reference :    3102**

If you make an error typing in this or any other entry then you can rectify the error using **BACKSPACE** . Pressing the **BACKSPACE** key causes the cursor to move back a character deleting the character as it does so. Press **BACKSPACE** until the cursor is at the beginning of the entry and type the entry in again.

When you have typed in the correct entry you must press **RETURN** to inform the system that your entry is complete. When you have done this a question appears at the bottom of the screen:

> **Is this a new account : No Yes**

It is, so select **Yes** by typing **Y** and the highlight moves opposite Account Name. Enter the name of the account as **STARTUP CAPITAL**.

> **Account Name     :    STARTUP CAPITAL**

Uppercase is not mandatory but it is consistent with the existing account names.

Remember to press **RETURN** to complete any entry. Leave the Yearly Budget and all the Month figures at 0.00 and press **ESC** to indicate that your entry is complete.

**Activity 4.2**    Post the Account to the ledger

Having pressed **ESC** at the end of the last Activity the following legend has appeared at the bottom of the screen:

### Do you want to : Post Edit Abandon

with a highlight on the default **Post**. Assuming you do not need to Edit your screen entry, you certainly do not wish to Abandon the entry so press **RETURN** to select the default Post and the Account will then be posted to the Nominal Ledger.

When the details you had typed into the screen clear, you are still in the Nominal Account Structure screen so press **ESC** to return to the Nominal Accounts screen and then **ESC** again to return to the Nominal Ledger screen.

---

**Activity 4.3**    Amend an existing Account

The Nominal Account BAD DEBT WRITE OFF has code 8100. You are going to set aside £3000 in this account to cater for any bad debts that may occur. This will mean retaining the Account Reference and Account Name but amending the Yearly Budget from the default of 0.00 to 3000.00. From the Nominal Ledger screen select Nominal Account Structure and from the Nominal Account Structure screen select Account Names to reveal the Nominal Accounts screen. Into this screen enter the Account Reference 8100:

### Account Reference :    8100

Immediately, the Account Name is displayed:

### Account Name    :    BAD DEBT WRITE OFF

Accept the default name and press **RETURN**. The highlight now moves to the Yearly Budget entry where you will type in 3000:

### Yearly Budget    :    3000.00

All the Month figures now change to 250.00 to permit the spreading of the budget load throughout the accounting year. When you are satisfied that all is correctly entered, press **ESC** to indicate that your entry is complete. At the prompt select Post to post your entry to the Nominal Ledger.

When the posting is complete press **ESC** twice to return to the Nominal Ledger screen.

**Activity 4.4**    View the new Accounts

From the Nominal Ledger screen select Accounts List and display the list of accounts on the screen. When the first 30 accounts appear on the screen press **RETURN** to display the next 30. You will see your new Account name in the top half of the left hand list. When you are satisfied that it has been posted correctly return to the Nominal Ledger screen and run off a new printed copy of the amended account codes. It is always useful to have a printed copy at hand when posting transactions to the ledgers. When the printing is complete press **ESC** to return to the Main Menu.

---

**Key words**    **Nominal Account Structure**
**Account Names**
**Adding an Account**
**BACKSPACE**
**Posting an Account**
**Amending an Account**

Task 5      **Entering the startup capital and bank loan**

**Objective**

To illustrate the use of Nominal Ledger codes and the posting of Bank receipts into the ledger.

**Instructions**

You are now ready to start setting up your ledger system for your company, Erin Fish Supplies. Display the Nominal Ledger screen and from this screen select Bank Transactions to display the Bank Transactions screen:

**Bank Payments**
**Bank Receipts**

---

**Activity 5.1**

Entering the formation capital Bank Receipt

Select Bank Receipts and the Bank Receipts screen appears. Enter the following information into this screen:

**N/C Bank :**    **1200**    This is the default code for the Bank Account. Accept it by pressing **RETURN** .

The name of the account is then automatically entered into the screen in replacement of the Nominal code 1200:

**N/C Bank :**    **BANK CURRENT ACCOUNT**

The cursor now moves to the left side of the screen below the heading **N/C**.

When posting transactions to ledgers it is necessary to have at hand a list of the Nominal Ledger Account codes. If, however, you have temporarily mislaid your printed copy Sage has provided a useful facility of allowing you to view them via the **F4** function key.

Press **F4** and there will be displayed all the Account names and codes. Press **PgDn** four times, after which the code 3102 STARTUP CAPITAL appears in the list. Move the highlight to this account using the cursor control keys. Press **RETURN** and the account code number is automatically entered into the screen as well as the account name STARTUP CAPITAL alongside N/C Name. Alternatively you could have just typed the number in. Complete the screen entry as follows:

| | | | |
|---|---|---|---|
| **N/C** | : | **3102** | STARTUP CAPITAL |
| **Dep** | : | **0** | *See page 94 for Departments* |
| **Date** | : | **010892** | 1 August 1992. (Press **F5** to have this automatically entered.) |
| **Cheque** | : | | This refers to the cheque number - leave blank as it has no bearing on your company. Press **RETURN** |
| **Details** | : | **Formation Capital** | |
| **Nett Amnt :** | | **12000.00** | |

| Tc | : | **T9** | This is the VAT tax code for a non-rated item. |
|---|---|---|---|
| **Tax Amnt** | : | **0.00** | There is no tax paid so the system calculates this to be zero. |

Press **RETURN** to move to the beginning of the next line.

Notice that the Batch Total at the top left hand corner of the screen now reads 12000.00 but the N/C Name at the top of the screen is now blank in readiness for another entry.

---

**Activity 5.2**

Entering the loan Bank Receipt

In addition to providing your own formation capital the company has taken out a loan to enable a van to be purchased. Enter the Bank Receipt details for the loan as follows:

> **N/C** : **2300**

Notice that the **N/C Name** now displays **LOANS.**

| **Dept** | : | **0** | |
|---|---|---|---|
| **Date** | : | **010892** | Again, press **F5** |
| **Cheque** | : | | Leave blank |
| **Details** | : | **Bank loan** | |
| **Nett Amnt** | : | **7000.00** | |
| **Tc** | : | **T9** | |
| **Tax Amnt** | : | **0.00** | Automatically calculated |

The Batch Total now reads 19000 - the sum of the two entries.

---

**Activity 5.3**

Posting the Bank Receipts to the Nominal Ledger

If you make an error at any time you can use the cursor control keys to move the highlight and overtype any individual entry. Try moving the highlight now.

All that you have done at the moment is to put information onto the screen. When you are satisfied that all the information entered is correct you must inform the system that it is complete by pressing **ESC**. Again you will be asked whether you wish to Post, Edit or Abandon your entry. Select Post and both bank receipts will be posted as:

> **Debit the Bank Account** by the gross amount (un-taxed value plus tax)
> **Credit the Nominal Accounts** by the appropriate un-taxed nett amounts.

Had there been a tax amount then this would have been posted to the Tax Control Account. Notice also, that when the posting is being executed a prompt appears at the bottom left of the screen:

## Updating Audit Trail ..

This is telling you that all necessary accounts are being updated.

When the posting is complete the Bank Receipts screen will clear all the details you had entered. Press **ESC** three times to return to the Main Menu.

| Key words | **Bank Receipts** |
|---|---|
| | **Entering a transaction** |
| | **N/C abbreviation for Nominal Code** |
| | **F4 function key** |
| | **F5 function key** |
| | **Post, Edit or Abandon** |
| | **Posting a transaction** |

# Setting up a supplier's details

**Objective**

To learn how to enter a supplier's name and address and account details into the system.

**Instructions**

You now have £19,000 in the bank and you need to purchase a refrigeration unit in which to keep your stock. This is a purchase and so the transaction will be recorded in the Purchase Ledger. Before we can enter a transaction into this ledger we must create a purchase ledger Account for the supplier of the refrigeration unit. Starting from the Main Menu select Purchase Ledger to display the Purchase Ledger screen:

**Supplier Details**
**Batched Data Entry**
**Payments**
**Refunds**
**Write Off Account**
**Address List**
**Account Balances (Aged)**
**Transaction History**
**Day Books**
**Remittance Advice Notes**
**Letters**

---

**Activity 6.1**

Enter Supplier Details

From the Purchase Ledger screen select Supplier Details and enter **FRIDGE** as listed.

**Account Reference :**    **FRIDGE**

This is the Purchase Ledger equivalent of a Nominal Ledger code. Such codes are not restricted to being numbers but can be a mixture of numbers and letters. When you have typed this entry and pressed **RETURN** the following prompt appears at the bottom of the screen:

**Is this a new account : No Yes**

Select **Yes** and enter the following into the rest of the screen:

| | | |
|---|---|---|
| **Account Name** | : | **ColdWare Ltd** |
| **Address** | : | **123 Ice Palace Road** |
| | : | **Bergton** |
| | : | **BE1 1EB** |
| | : | |
| **Credit Limit** | : | **0.00** |
| **Turnover** | : | **0.00** |
| | | |
| **Telephone No** | : | **0123 456789** |

| Contact Name | : | **Jack Frost** |
| **Discount Code** | : | Leave blank |
| **Analysis Code** | : | Leave blank |

For those items that are left at the default 0.00 or are left blank, just press **RETURN** to accept the default and to move to the next entry space.

---

**Activity 6.2**     Posting the supplier details

When you are satisfied that the details entered are correct press **ESC** to complete the entry. At the prompt select Post and your supplier details entry will be posted to the Purchase Ledger leaving a blank Supplier Details screen in readiness for the entry of another Supplier. Press **ESC** to return to the Purchase Ledger screen.

---

**Key words**     **Supplier Details**
                  **Account Reference**

# Entering a purchase invoice

**Objective**

To learn how to post a purchase invoice into the Purchase Ledger.

**Instructions**

Having established a Supplier Account we can now record transactions between the company and the supplier in that account. The company has purchased a refrigeration unit from ColdWare Ltd at a cost of £3,600 and a purchase invoice has been received from them. The details of this purchase invoice must now be posted into the Purchase Ledger. From the Purchase Ledger screen select Batched Data Entry to display the Batched Data Entry screen:

> **Purchase Invoices**
> **Purchase Credit notes**

Select Purchase Invoices and display the Purchase Invoices screen.

---

**Activity 7.1**

Entering the purchase invoice details

The highlight for information entry into the Purchase Invoices entry screen is beneath the heading A/C. Into the Purchase Invoices screen enter the following details:

| | | | |
|---|---|---|---|
| **A/C** | : | **FRIDGE** | This connects with the supplier account |

Notice that the name ColdWare Ltd appears automatically at the top of the screen alongside A/C Name.

| | | | |
|---|---|---|---|
| **Date** | : | **010892** | Press **F5** |
| **Inv** | : | **773** | This is ColdWare's invoice number |
| **N/C** | : | **0020** | PLANT AND MACHINERY Nominal Account |

Notice that the legend PLANT AND MACHINERY appears at the top of the screen alongside the N/C Name. Details from this purchase invoice will also be posted to this Nominal account automatically.

| | | | |
|---|---|---|---|
| **Dept** | : | **0** | |
| **Details** | : | **Refrigeration unit** | |
| **Nett Amnt** | : | **3600** | |
| **Tc** | : | **T1** | This is the ordinary rate of VAT (17.5%) |
| **Tax Amnt** | : | **630.00** | This is calculated automatically by the system. |

Press **RETURN** to place the highlight at the beginning of a new line.

| | |
|---|---|
| **Activity 7.2** | Posting the purchase invoice to the Purchase Ledger |

When you are satisfied that the details entered into the Purchase Invoices screen are correct press **ESC** to tell the system that your entry is complete. At the prompt select Post and purchase invoice details will be posted as:

**Credit the Creditor's Control Account** by the gross amount
**Debit the Nominal Account 0020** by the nett amount
**Debit the Tax Control Account** by the tax amount

Notice again, that when the posting is being executed a prompt appears at the bottom left of the screen:

**Updating Audit Trail ..**

This is telling you that all necessary accounts are being updated.
When the details of the purchase invoice clear from the screen press **ESC** twice to return to the Purchase Ledger screen.

| | |
|---|---|
| **Key words** | **Purchase invoice**<br>**T1 standard tax rate**<br>**Creditor's Control Account**<br>**Tax Control Account** |

Task 8

# Issuing a remittance advice note and paying a purchase invoice

**Objective**

To learn how to issue a remittance advice note and post a purchase invoice payment into the system.

**Instructions**

The refrigeration unit was purchased from ColdWare without any credit arrangements and so the purchase invoice was paid when the unit was delivered. We must now post this payment into the Purchase Ledger. When you send a cheque to a supplier in payment for a delivery it is your customary practice to accompany the cheque with a remittance advice note that tells your supplier exactly what the cheque is for. When executing this payment procedure the remittance advice note must be issued before the payment is posted to the bank account. If you post the payment first then the system will not issue a remittance advice note. From the Purchase Ledger screen select Remittance Advice Notes to display the Remittance Advice Notes screen.

---

**Activity 8.1**

Issuing a remittance advice note

The Remittance Advice Notes screen will require your response to six questions. Respond as follows:

| | | |
|---|---|---|
| **Lower Account Reference   000000** | : | **FRIDGE** |
| **Upper Account Reference   FRIDGE** | : | Press **RETURN** |
| **Enter Date of Report** | : | **010892** |
| **Printer or File** | : | **P** for printer |
| **Print Individual Items** | : | **Y** |
| **Your Address on Stationery** | : | **Y** |

The message:

**Switch the Printer On and Press RETURN**

appears. Press **RETURN** and the remittance advice note will be printed out showing the date of payment, your supplier's invoice number, the invoice details and the gross amount.

---

```
ColdWare Ltd                               FRIDGE
123 Ice Palace Road
Bergton                                    010892
BE1 1EB


010892      773      Refrigeration unit              4230.00
```

**Activity 8.2**

Posting the purchase invoice payment

From the Purchase Ledger screen select Payments to display the Payments screen. Enter the payment details of the purchase invoice as listed into the Payments screen:

| | | | |
|---|---|---|---|
| **N/C Bank** | : | **1200** | Accept the default by pressing **RETURN** |
| **A/C Ref.** | : | **FRIDGE** | |
| **Payment Date** | : | **010892** | Press **F5** |
| **Cheque Number** | : | **1** | |

Notice the display on the top right is showing the Account Name as ColdWare Ltd and the highlight is now opposite Cheque Amount. You are now required to enter the amount that you paid for the refrigeration unit. We shall assume that you have temporarily mislaid the documentation but you remember that you paid £3600 for the unit. What you cannot remember is the VAT amount. No problem. Press **F2** and the calculator comes into view. Enter the following sequence of symbols into the calculator (notice that ⁎ stands for multiplication):

**3600 ⁎ 1.175 =**

The calculator display then shows **4230** - the total value of the purchase invoice. Press **RETURN** and this value is automatically entered as the Cheque Amount. Press **RETURN** again and immediately the screen displays the details from the purchase invoice. Notice the Cheque Balance which also reads **4230**. Under the heading Tp are the letters **PI**. These refer to the fact that the transaction is going to pay a Purchase Invoice. At the bottom of the screen is the legend:

**Method of payment :   Automatic Manual**

Select Manual by typing **M** . When you have done this the details of the Purchase Invoice to be paid, as displayed on the screen, are completely highlighted. Press **RETURN** again and you are then asked the question:

**Type of payment : Full Part Discount Cancel**

You can now pay the invoice in full, in part, at a discounted rate or cancel the payment.

You wish to pay the invoice in full so select the default Full by pressing **RETURN**. The word FULL appears beneath the heading Payment. Now press **ESC** to complete your entry. At the prompt select Post and the payment will be posted as:

**Debit the Creditor's Control Account** by the payment
**Credit the Bank Account** by the payment

Again you will see the audit trail update message.

When the posting is complete you will be returned to a blank Payments screen. Press **ESC** twice to return to the Main Menu.

---

| Key words | **Remittance advice note** |
|---|---|
| | **Payments screen** |
| | **Posting a payment** |
| | **Manual posting** |
| | **Full payment** |

19

# The Transaction and Control Account Histories

**Objective**  To appreciate some of the standard reporting facilities offered by the system.

**Instructions**  From the Main Menu select Nominal Ledger.

---

**Activity 9.1**  Viewing the Transaction History in the Nominal Ledger

From the Nominal Ledger screen select Transaction History and on the Transaction History screen enter:

| | | | |
|---|---|---|---|
| **Lower Account Reference** | **000000** | : | Press **RETURN** |
| **Upper Account Reference** | **999999** | : | Press **RETURN** |
| **Display, Printer or File** | **D** | : | Press **RETURN** |

The transactions will now be displayed for each Nominal Account reference code at a time in the numerical order of their Nominal Account code. The first to be displayed is the third transaction entered into the system; the payment for the refrigeration unit with Nominal Account code 0020. Beneath the heading Tp (Type of transaction) are the letters PI. These refer to the type of transaction being a Purchase Invoice. Press **RETURN** and the second transaction displayed is the payment into the bank of the loan with Nominal Account code 2300. Notice that beneath Tp are the letters BR which refer to Bank Receipt. Press **RETURN** again and the third transaction displayed is the payment into the bank of the Formation Capital with Nominal Code 3102.

Press **ESC** to exit the Transaction History screen and return to the Nominal Ledger screen.

---

**Activity 9.2**  Viewing the Bank Account history

From the Nominal Ledger screen select Control Account History to display the Control Account History screen.

> **Debtor's Control**
> **Creditor's Control**
> **Bank Accounts**
> **Petty Cash**
> **Tax Control**

Here you see a number of Control Accounts listed. Select Bank Accounts and into the Bank Accounts screen enter:

**Bank Account Code**     **1200**   :   Press **RETURN**

**Lower Transaction No.**   **1**   :   Press **RETURN**

**Upper Transaction No.**   **4**   :   Press **RETURN**

**Display, Printer or File**   **D**   :   Press **RETURN**

The display shows the three bank transactions with a final balance in the bank of £14,770.00. The number 1 beneath Ref. for the purchase payment refers to the cheque number.

| No. | Tp | Date | Ref | Details | Value | Debit | Credit |
|---|---|---|---|---|---|---|---|
| 1 | BR | 010892 | | Formation Capital | 12000.00 | | |
| 2 | BR | 010892 | | Bank loan | 7000.00 | 19000.00 | |
| 4 | PP | 010892 | 1 | Purchase Payment | 4230.00 | | 4230.00 |
| | | | | | Totals : | 19000.00 | 4230.00 |
| | | | | | Balance : | 14770.00 | |

The letters PP beneath Tp for the third transaction in the list refer to Purchase Payment. Notice that payment into the bank is recorded as a Debit to the Bank Account and payment out as a Credit to the Bank Account.

When you feel that you appreciate all the information displayed on this screen press **ESC** to return to the Control Account History screen.

---

**Activity 9.3**     Viewing the Creditor's Control Account

From the Control Account History screen select Creditor's Control. Accept the three defaults in the creditor's Control screen, after which you will see the value of the Refrigeration Unit (the gross amount paid for it) as a Credit to the account and the actual payment for the unit as a Debit to the account. Notice that the Credit balances the Debit as shown by the Balance figure of 0.00.

When you feel that you appreciate all the information displayed on this screen press **ESC** to return to the Control Account History screen.

---

**Activity 9.4**     Viewing the Tax Control Account History

From the Control Account History screen select Tax Control and display the Tax Control screen. Again, accept the four default values displayed on the Tax Control screen to display the Tax Control history which records the £630 VAT paid on the refrigeration unit.

| No. | Tp | Date | Ref | Details | Value | Debit | Credit |
|-----|-----|--------|-----|-------------------|--------|--------|--------|
| 3 | PI | 010892 | 773 | Refrigeration unit | 630.00 | 630.00 | |
| | | | | Totals : | | 630.00 | 0.00 |
| | | | | Balance : | | 630.00 | |

Notice that from Activities 9.1 and 9.2 the payment of £4230 recorded as a Credit in the Bank Account is balanced by the £3600 Debit in the Nominal Account 0020 and the £630 Debit in the Tax Control Account.

When you feel that you appreciate all the information displayed on this screen press **ESC** twice to return to the Nominal Ledger screen.

---

**Key words**

**Transaction history**
**Control Account**
**Bank Account history**
**Creditor's Control Account history**
**Tax Account history**

Task 10

# The bank receipt Day Book and the Trial Balance

**Objective**    To appreciate the Day Book structure and to learn how to obtain a Trial Balance.

**Instructions**    The Day Books facility permits you to view a list of transactions entered within a specific period and the Sales, Purchase and Nominal Ledgers all have associated Day Books. The Trial Balance facility provides a check that the Nominal Accounts do balance.

Ensure that the Nominal Ledger screen is on display.

---

**Activity 10.1**    Viewing the Nominal Ledger Day Books

From the Nominal Ledger screen select Day Books to display the Nominal Day Books screen:

**Bank Payments**
**Bank Receipts**
**Cash Payments**
**Cash Receipts**
**Journal Entries**

Here you will see five Day Books listed. Select Bank Receipts and accept all five defaults on the Bank Receipts screen to view the Bank receipt history. This shows the two bank receipts of £12000 and £7000.

| No. | Tp | A/C | N/C | Date | Ref. | Details | Net Amnt | Tax Amnt |
|-----|----|----|-----|------|------|---------|----------|----------|
| 1 | BR | 1200 | 3102 | 010892 | | Formation Capital | 12000.00 | 0.00 |
| 2 | BR | 1200 | 2300 | 010892 | | Bank loan | 7000.00 | 0.00 |
| | | | | | | | 19000.00 | 0.00 |

Press **ESC** twice to return to the Nominal Ledger screen.

---

**Activity 10.2**    Viewing the Trial Balance

From the Nominal Ledger screen select Trial Balance and display the current state of the company.

| Ref. | Accounts Name | Debit | Credit |
|------|---------------|-------|--------|
| 0020 | PLANT AND MACHINERY | 3600.00 | |
| 1200 | BANK CURRENT ACCOUNT | 14770.00 | |
| 2200 | TAX CONTROL ACCOUNT | 630.00 | |
| 2300 | LOANS | | 7000.00 |
| 3102 | STARTUP CAPITAL | | 12000.00 |

At the bottom of the screen the totals are displayed:

| | | | |
|--|--|--|--|
| | | 19000.00 | 19000.00 |

This shows that the Debits balance the Credits. Press **ESC** twice to return to the Main Menu.

---

| Key words | Day Books |
|-----------|-----------|
| | Trial Balance |

# Task 11     Journal entry of a van purchase

**Objective**

To be able to enter a purchase and payment into the Nominal Ledger without using the Purchase Ledger.

**Instructions**

Your company has bought a van to enable deliveries to be made. This was bought on the mainland from a secondhand car dealer with no servicing facilities. As a consequence you will probably never have any further dealings with that company so there is no need to set up a Purchase Account for it. The purchase and payment transactions must, however be posted to the Nominal Ledger. Because you will not be posting via the Purchase Ledger you will have to post directly into the Nominal Ledger. Such postings are called Journal Entries and must be performed with caution. Any posting to the Nominal Ledger must have a balancing Debit and Credit. Ordinarily, when posting via the Purchase Ledger such balancing is performed by the Control Accounts and you need not concern yourself with the intricacies. However, when posting directly into the Nominal Ledger it is best to write out the posting on a sheet of paper first.

---

**Activity 11.1**

Preparing for a Journal Entry

The company has purchased a van costing £8000 plus VAT at 17.5%, giving a total payment of:

### £8000 + £1400 = £9400

You might check this figure using the calculator. Press **F2** to display the calculator and enter the number 8000. Press **✕** followed by 1.175 and then **=** . The display then shows the correct result 9400. Press **ESC** to remove the calculator. This purchase must be entered as:

### £9400 Credit Nominal Code 1200 for BANK CURRENT ACCOUNT
### £8000 Debit Nominal Code 0050 for MOTOR VEHICLES
### £1400 Debit Nominal Code 2200 for TAX CONTROL ACCOUNT

You are now ready to post these details as a Journal Entry.

---

**Activity 11.2**

Making a Journal Entry

Display the Nominal Ledger screen and select Journal Entries. Enter the Date by pressing **F5** and the highlight moves to Reference. Type in **VanPur** to represent the van purchase and to identify the Journal Entry.

Press **RETURN** and enter the debit and credit as described in the following:

| N/C | Dep. | Details | Tc | Debit | Credit |
|-----|------|---------|-----|---------|---------|
| 1200 | 0 | Van Purchase | T9 | | 9400.00 |
| 0050 | 0 | Untaxed van | T1 | 8000.00 | |
| 2200 | 0 | Tax paid for van | T1 | 1400.00 | |

Notice the Nominal Account code 2200. This is reserved for Tax and must be used whenever tax is entered in this way.

When you have completed the entry notice that the Batch Total is zero. This means that the Nominal Ledger entry that you are proposing to make does indeed balance because the two Debit values add up to the Credit value. If it did not balance then the system would not let you make the posting.

Having achieved a balance press **ESC** to indicate to the system that your entry is complete. At the prompt press **P** to post the entry. When the posting is complete press **ESC** to return to the Nominal Ledger screen.

You may now wish to look through the various reports available from the Nominal Ledger screen to see the effect of the posting you have just made.

| Key words | Journal Entry |
|-----------|---------------|
| | **Balancing the Nominal Ledger** |
| | **Debit and Credit** |

Task 12          **Setting up the van loan prepayments**

**Objective**       To learn how to spread a one-off payment through the accounting year.

**Instructions**    Your arrangements with the bank when your company borrowed £7000 to enable it to
                    buy a van was that the company would pay interest only at 18% for the full year and at
                    the year end would pay off the outstanding loan amount of £7000. We shall consider the
                    interest payments in the next Task and here we shall be concerned with the normal
                    accounting practice of spreading a load. The outstanding amount of £7000 which is due
                    to be paid in a year's time will be accounted for in twelve equal monthly installments each
                    of which will be automatically posted to the Nominal Ledger every month as a Prepayment
                    during the Month End procedure. The facility to set up Prepayments and Accruals is
                    available from within the Nominal Ledger under Prepayments and Accruals.

---

**Activity 12.1**    Setting up a prepayment

                    From the Nominal Ledger screen select Prepayments and Accruals. From the Prepayments
                    and Accruals screen select Prepayments and enter the following details:

| | | | |
|---|---|---|---|
| **Name** | : | **Van loan repayment** | |
| **N/C** | : | **2300** | The LOANS Nominal Ledger code |
| **PRP** | : | **1103** | The PREPAYMENTS Nominal Ledger Account code. Press **RETURN** to accept the default. |
| **Value** | : | **7000.00** | |
| **Mth** | : | **12** | Spread over 12 months |
| **Pst** | : | **0** | The number of payments already posted |
| **Monthly Jrn** | : | **583.33** | The actual value posted each month. This is automatically calculated by the system |
| **P** | : | | Leave blank. This shows a star when the current month's payment has been made. |

                    Press **ESC** to confirm your entry and at the prompt select Post. When you do this the
                    details of the prepayments are stored in a file on your disk but no transactions are posted
                    to the ledgers. The information that you have entered is simply recorded for use at a later
                    time when the details are posted to the ledgers during the Month End procedures.

---

**Activity 12.2**    Setting up additional prepayments

                    In addition to the van loan repayment you will have other lump sums to pay for at other
                    times during the year. Your total insurance commitment of £250 becomes due in six
                    months time and the company is committed to a van service in nine months time that is set

at £125, both items attracting VAT at the standard rate. Set up two more prepayments to spread this load - the first over six months and the second over nine months. Use Nominal Ledger codes 8204 for the INSURANCE; 7301 (REPAIRS AND SERVICING) for the van service. Use the calculator (**F2**) to work out the totals due. For example, for the van service:

$$125 * 1.175 = 146.875$$

and press **RETURN** to place this figure into the Prepayments screen. Notice that when you enter the 146.875 from the calculator into the Prepayments screen the amount is rounded to 146.88 When your entry is complete and saved to the disk file, press **ESC** twice to return to the Nominal Ledger screen.

Notice that when you enter these two additional prepayments the screen also displays the first prepayment for the bank loan. When you post these entries you do not end up with two postings of the first entry because the second posting overwrites the first on the disk.

| Key words | **Spreading the load** |
| | **Prepayments** |

Task 13　　　**Accounting for recurring entries**

**Objective**　　To learn how to set up recurring entries that are posted automatically at the end of each month during the Month End procedure.

**Instructions**　　At 18% per annum the interest on the £7000 loan runs at £105 per month. It has been agreed to pay this by standing order and this recurring transaction must now be accounted for.

---

**Activity 13.1**　　Setting up recurring entries for van loan interest

From the Nominal Ledger screen select Recurring Entries and enter the following details into the Recurring Entries screen:

| | | | |
|---|---|---|---|
| **Tp** | : | **BP** | Bank Payment |
| **N/C** | : | **7900** | BANK INTEREST PAID Nominal Account code |
| **Date** | : | **TODAY** | This is entered by pressing the **F5** function key. It ensures that the transaction will be posted when the posting routine is set into operation and will not require the date to be changed each month. |
| **Ref** | : | | Leave blank |
| **Bank** | : | **1200** | |
| **Dep** | : | **O** | |
| **Details** | : | **Bank loan interest** | |
| **Nett Amnt** | : | **105.00** | |
| **Tc** | : | **T9** | Bank interest is not rated for VAT and not rated items are coded T9 |
| **Tax Amnt** | : | **0.00** | |

When you are satisfied that your entry is correct press **ESC** and from the prompt select Post. When you do this the details of the prepayments are stored in a file on your disk but no transactions are posted to the ledgers. The information that you have entered is simply recorded for use at a later time when the details are posted to the ledgers during the Month End procedures.

---

**Activity 13.2**　　Setting up additional recurring entries

In addition to the van loan interest you will have electricity and telephone to pay for. Under prearranged terms you have agreed to pay £80 per month for your electricity and £75 per month for your telephone. Both of these are rated at the standard rate of VAT. Use Nominal Ledger codes 7200 for electricity and 7502 for telephone and set up two additional recurring entries for these transactions.

Notice that when you enter these two additional recurring entries the screen also displays the first recurring entry for bank interest. When you post these entries you do not end up with two postings of the first entry because the second posting overwrites the first on the disk.

| Key words | Recurring entries |
|-----------|-------------------|

## Task 14

**Objective**

To learn how to cater for asset depreciation.

**Instructions**

Erin Fish Supplies is now the proud possessor of a refrigeration unit and a van. These two items are assets and like all assets of this nature they lose value as time progresses. This loss of value - or depreciation - can be accounted for within the Sage Sterling Accounting system by using the Depreciation facility offered within the Nominal Ledger.

## Setting up asset depreciation

---

**Activity 14.1**

To post asset depreciation

From the Nominal Ledger screen select the Depreciation option and enter the following:

| | | | |
|---|---|---|---|
| **Name** | : | **Refrigeration unit** | |
| **N/C** | : | **0021** | PLANT AND MACHINERY DEPRECIATION |
| **Value** | : | **3600.00** | |
| **Tp** | : | **R** | Reducing balance, the value reducing by a set percentage each year |
| **%** | : | **15.00** | 15% reduction in value from previous year's value |
| **Amount** | : | **48.43** | The amount of next month's depreciation. This is calculated automatically by the system. |
| **Current** | : | **3600.00** | Automatically entered by the system. |
| **P** | : | | A star will appear here to indicate that this item has been posted for the current month |

When you are satisfied that the details are correct press **ESC** and at the prompt select Post. When you do this the details of the prepayments are stored in a file on your disk but no transactions are posted to the ledgers. The information that you have entered is simply recorded for use at a later time when the details are posted to the ledgers during the Month End procedures.

---

**Activity 14.2**

To post a further asset depreciation

The van, currently valued at £8000, is liable to an annual straight line depreciation (coded by the letter S) of 25% of the original value each year. Use the Nominal Code 0051 for MOTOR VEHICLE DEPRECIATION and post this asset's depreciation to the disk file.

Notice that when you enter this additional depreciation the screen also displays the first depreciation for the refrigeration unit. When you post these entries you do not end up with two postings of the first entry because the second posting overwrites the first on the disk.

When your entries are complete and posted, press **ESC** to return to the Main Menu.

# Section B: Starting the first month's trading ▬

Having set up your accounting system you are now going to enter some sale and purchase transactions. You will enter your purchases into stock and you will issue invoices and abstract your sales from stock. In addition you will produce statements and remittance advices for onward transmission to your customers.

The following table describes which of the Tasks in this Section are available in which component of the Sage Sterling Accounting system:

| Task | 15 | 16 | 17 | 18 | 19 | 20 | 21 | 22 | 23 |
|------|-----|-----|-----|-----|-----|-----|-----|-----|-----|
| Bookkeeper | yes | yes | no | no | yes | no | no | no | no |
| Accountant | yes | yes | no | no | yes | no | no | no | yes |
| Accountant + | yes | yes | yes | yes | yes | yes | yes | yes | yes |
| Financial Controller | yes | yes | yes | yes | yes | yes | yes | yes | yes |

Task 15

# Setting up further supplier details

**Objective**

To reinforce and test the ability to set up supplier details and to learn how to post opening balances.

**Instructions**

Before Erin Fish Supplies can begin making a profit it must have some stock to sell. The company already has a number of suppliers with whom it has been dealing in the past. Accounts containing the names and addresses of these suppliers need to be created in the Purchase Ledger. In addition, because the company still owes some of them money from purchases made prior to 1 August 1992 we must also record their Opening Balances. Ensure that the Main Menu is being displayed and from this menu select the Purchase Ledger.

---

**Activity 15.1**

Entering further supplier details

You have already seen how to enter supplier details in Task 6. To give you more practice in performing this operation select Supplier Details from the Purchase Ledger screen and enter the following suppliers into the Purchase Ledger.

Remember to press **RETURN** after you have entered the Analysis Code otherwise it will not be retained for posting.

|  |  |  |
|---|---|---|
| **Account Reference** | : | **WILL** |

You do not need to use the **SHIFT** key here. The account reference entry automatically enters in capital letters.

| | | |
|---|---|---|
| **Account Name** | : | **P Williams** |
| **Address** | : | **4 Front View** |
| | : | **Seaporth** |
| | : | **SE2 1LI** |
| | : | |
| | | |
| **Credit Limit** | : | **0.00** |
| **Turnover** | : | **0.00** |
| | | |
| **Telephone** | : | 0345 678912 |
| **Contact Name** | : | Phil |
| **Discount Code** | : | |
| **Analysis Code** | : | **S1** |

Remember to press **ESC** when the entry is complete to Post the entry to the Ledger. Continue entering the following:

| | | |
|---|---|---|
| Account Reference | : | HISEA |
| Account Name | : | MV Hisea |
| Address | : | Berth 2 |
| | : | Canary Dock |
| | : | Upton-on-Sea |
| | : | UP1 2WQ |
| | | |
| Credit Limit | : | 2000.00 |
| Turnover | : | 0.00 |
| | | |
| Telephone | : | 0456 789123 |
| Contact Name | : | Rod |
| Discount Code | : | |
| Analysis Code | : | S2 |

| | | |
|---|---|---|
| Account Reference | : | ABC |
| Account Name | : | ABC Fishery |
| Address | : | Shark House |
| | : | 35 Myrtle Street |
| | : | Atlantica |
| | : | AL3 6VH |
| | | |
| Credit Limit | : | 3000.00 |
| Turnover | : | 0.00 |
| | | |
| Telephone | : | 0567 891234 |
| Contact Name | : | Jack |
| Discount Code | : | |
| Analysis Code | : | S3 |

| | | |
|---|---|---|
| Account Reference | : | SMILE |
| Account Name | : | H Smiley |
| Address | : | Seacroft |
| | : | Shell Terrace |
| | : | Sewed |
| | : | SE4 9OP |
| | | |
| Credit Limit | : | 0.00 |
| Turnover | : | 0.00 |
| | | |
| Telephone | : | 0678 912345 |
| Contact Name | : | Theo |
| Discount Code | : | |
| Analysis Code | : | S4 |

| Account Reference | : | WOOD |
| --- | --- | --- |
| Account Name | : | T Feller |
| Address | : | Dark Wood |
| | : | Glade Green |
| | : | Timberland |
| | : | T1 1T |
| | | |
| Credit Limit | : | 1000.00 |
| Turnover | : | 0.00 |
| | | |
| Telephone | : | 0789 123456 |
| Contact Name | : | Pan |
| Discount Code | : | |
| Analysis Code | : | S5 |

Notice the amounts listed under Credit Limit. This refers to the credit the supplier has given to your company. These accounts are monthly accounts and must be settled by the fifteenth day of the month following delivery. For those suppliers giving no credit the terms are cash on delivery. By cash it will be understood that a cheque will suffice. We shall deal with the handling of cash later in the *Guide*.

Each supplier also has an Analysis Code listed. These range from S1 to S5 and we shall see the use that these can be put to later in the *Guide*.

When you have posted the details of the last supplier press **ESC** to return to the Purchase Ledger screen.

---

**Activity 15.2**    Posting Opening Balances

Posting opening balances follows the same procedure used to enter purchase invoices which you have already done in Task 7. The only difference is in the references used. From the Purchase Ledger screen select Batched Data Entry. From the Batched Data Entry screen select Purchase Invoices and enter the following two opening balances (when you are entering the details for the WOOD account press the **F6** function key to duplicate the entry in the line above when the entry in the line above is to be the same as that in the line below):

| A/C | Date | Inv | N/C | Dep | Details | Nett Amnt | Tc | Tax Amnt |
| --- | --- | --- | --- | --- | --- | --- | --- | --- |
| HISEA | 010892 | O/Bal | 9998 | 0 | Opening balance | 854.79 | T0 | 0.00 |
| WOOD | 010892 | O/Bal | 9998 | 0 | Opening balance | 132.64 | T1 | 23.21 |

The Nominal Ledger code 9998 is called the SUSPENSE ACCOUNT and is used only for opening balances. Notice also the Invoice reference of O/Bal *which must also always be used for opening balances.*

When you are satisfied that your screen entry is correct press **ESC** and Post the transactions. When the Purchase Invoices screen clears, press **ESC** twice to return to the Purchase Ledger screen.

**Key words**    **SUSPENSE ACCOUNT 9998**
**Opening balances**
**Invoice code O/Bal**
**Credit Limit**
**Monthly account**
**Cash on delivery**

# Entering and paying further purchase invoices

**Objective**

To reinforce and test the ability to post purchase invoices and their payments.

**Instructions**

Having opened the supplier accounts we must now post the company's purchases to their respective accounts and, for those suppliers that do not give the company credit, we must also post the payments for the purchases. Both of these procedures you have already performed in Tasks 7 and 8.

Whenever purchase invoices are to be posted it is good practice to check the figures on the invoice to see that no error has been made. You can use the Calculator that is accessible using the **F2** key to do this.

---

**Activity 16.1**

Posting further purchase invoices

From the Purchase Ledger screen select Batched Data Entry and post the following purchase invoices using the Nominal Account name STOCK with code 1001 and Department 1 for Timber, Department 2 for Scallops and Department 3 for Oysters (we shall look at departments in more detail later in the *Guide*):

**Purchase Invoice No. 124**

**T Feller**
**Dark Wood**
**Glade Green**
**Timberland T1 1T**                                          Date: 5 Aug 92

**Supply to Erin Fish Supplies**

**25 Tonnes cut timber @ £15.00 per tonne**

|        |   |      £ |
|--------|---|-------:|
| Value  | : | 375.00 |
| VAT    | : |  65.63 |
| Total  | : | 440.63 |

**Terms: Monthly Account**

**Purchase Invoice No. 003042**

**MV Hisea**
**Berth 2**
**Canary Dock**
**Upton-on-Sea UP1 2WQ**                                      Date: 4 Aug 92

**Supply to Erin Fish Supplies**

**250 dozen scallops @ £6.00 per dozen**

|  |  | **£** |
|---|---|---|
| Value | : | 1500.00 |
| VAT | : | 0.00 |
| Total | : | 1500.00 |

**Terms Monthly Account**

**Purchase Invoice No. 2771**

**P Williams**
**4 Front View**
**Seaporth SE2 1LI**                              **Date: 9 Aug 92**

**Supply to Erin Fish Supplies**

**10,000 oysters @ £0.25 each**

|  |  | **£** |
|---|---|---|
| Value | : | 2500.00 |
| VAT | : | 0.00 |
| Total | : | 2500.00 |

**Terms: COD**

Note the abbreviation COD for Cash On Delivery.

---

| **Activity 16.2** | Posting payments for further purchase invoices |
|---|---|

Because the invoice from P Williams was issued under the terms of cash on delivery this order was paid for when it was delivered. This payment will now have to be posted to the Purchase Ledger. You have already followed this procedure in Task 8. Select Payments from the Purchase Ledger screen and post the payment of £2500 in respect of P Williams' invoice number 2771 - the cheque number that you used is 2. Choose Automatic Payment. The details are then highlighted and the word FULL appears beneath Payment. Press **ESC** and from the prompt select Post. When the posting is complete press **ESC** twice to return to the Main Menu.

# Setting up the stock categories

**Objective**        To learn how to assign Categories to stock.

**Instructions**     The company possesses a refrigeration unit to store fish and a yard to store timber. This is physical stock holding. The Sage Sterling Accounting system has a facility for keeping a record of stock and this is accessible from the Main Menu. Just as accounts are given a code so stock items are coded into Categories and before we can begin to account for stock held we must set up these Categories. Display the Main Menu and select Stock Control to display the Stock Control screen:

> **Update Stock Details**
> **Categories**
> **Adjustments In**
> **Adjustments Out**
> **Stock Transfers**
> **Stock Details**
> **Stock History**
> **Stock Valuation**
> **Profit Report**
> **Stock Explosion**
> **Re-Order levels**

---

**Activity 17.1**        Setting up the stock categories

From the Stock Control screen select Categories and enter the following category names:

> **Category Name   1   :   Timber**
> **"        "        2   :   Fish**

Press **ESC** to post these categories and to return to the Stock Control screen. We are now ready to enter stock details.

---

**Key words**        **Stock Control**
                     **Categories**

## Task 18 — Entering purchases into stock

**Objective**

To learn how to post purchases into stock.

**Instructions**

All purchases are sold on from stock. The company has a refrigeration unit to store fish stock and a yard to store the timber. However, there will be many times when the company will make a sale without actually having had a delivery. For example, you may find a customer for timber on the mainland so it would be counter productive to have the timber delivered to the island only to send it back to the mainland again. As a consequence the timber would not have been physically stored as stock. However, despite this fact proper accounting procedure requires that you enter the timber as stock so that the purchase transaction shows it being put into accounted stock and the subsequent sale transaction shows it as being accounted for out of stock.

There are two stages in recording the purchases of new stock items:

(a) All the details relating to the description of the stock are recorded with the exception of the quantity to be put into stock

(b) The quantity of stock is then recorded as having been put into stock

We have three purchases to enter into stock. From the Main Menu select Stock Control to display the Stock Control screen.

---

**Activity 18.1**

Posting the timber details to stock

From the Stock Control screen select Update Stock Details to display the Update Stock Details screen. This screen requires all the details relating to individual stock items but not all of the details can be entered at the moment.

Enter the following information into this screen:

| | | | |
|---|---|---|---|
| **Stock Code** | : | **CT** | This refers to Cut Timber |
| **Description** | : | **Cut timber** | |
| **Category** | : | **1** | |
| **Category Name** | : | **Timber** | This appears automatically |
| **Sale Price** | : | **30.00** | |
| **Cost Price** | : | **0.00** | The system will not let you enter this yet |
| **Unit of Sale** | : | **Tonne** | |
| **Re-order level** | : | **5.00** | This is the level of stock at which a re-order should be made |
| **Re-order qty** | : | **25.00** | This is the default quantity that should be ordered |
| **Discount A%** | : | **5.00** | |
| **Discount B%** | : | **0.00** | |
| **Discount C%** | : | **0.00** | |
| **Nominal Code** | : | **1001** | |
| **Department** | : | **1** | |
| **Tax Code** | : | **T1** | |

At this point the highlight jumps to Make Up and refuses to move when you press **RETURN** . Press the **DOWN ARROW** to move the highlight to Supplier.

| | | | |
|---|---|---|---|
| **Supplier** | : | **WOOD** | |
| **Part Ref.** | : | | Leave blank |
| **Location** | : | **Yard** | This displays where the stock item is to be physically found |

Leave all other items as their default value displays.

Notice the Discount A% has been entered as 5%. If a customer is sufficiently valued to warrant a discount on his purchases then this value can be automatically applied to his invoice as we shall see in a later Task.

When you press **RETURN** after typing in Yard for Location you are confronted by a second screen display. This relates to the construction of stock items from components and does not have any relevance to the current Activity. Press **ESC** to return to the original screen and then press **ESC** again to display the prompt:

### Do you want to : Post Abandon Delete

in the top right hand corner of the screen.

When you are satisfied that these details are complete select Post to post these details to the stock file. When the Update Stock Details screen clears press **ESC** to return to the Stock Control Screen.

You will notice that you have not entered the quantity delivered into stock. Indeed, it is not possible to do so at this stage. Just as the Nominal Ledger has to balance so the Stock Control system has to reflect true inputs and true outputs with no possibilities of error. This means that the only way you can enter stock quantities into the Stock Control system is via one of the following procedures:

| | |
|---|---|
| **Adjustment IN** | to increase the stock level |
| **Adjustment OUT** | to decrease the stock level |
| **Despatch Sales order** | to decrease the stock level |
| **Receive Purchase order** | to increase the stock level |

The latter two methods can be performed only if your system possess the Financial Controller facility. In such a situation the stock is changed automatically by the system as we shall see in a later Task. The first two methods permit manual change of stock and must be used if your system does not possess the Financial Controller facility.

---

**Activity 18.2**

Posting the purchased timber quantity to stock

From the Stock Control screen select Adjustments In and the Adjustments In screen is displayed:

Enter the following information into this screen:

| Stock Code | : | CT | |
|---|---|---|---|
| Quantity | : | 25 | |
| Cost Price | : | 15.00 | Now the cost price is entered |
| Narrative | : | Delivery | |

The default entry here is Opening stock. Press the **DELETE** key and hold it down until the default entry is erased and then overtype the new entry.

| Reference | : | WOOD |
|---|---|---|
| Date | : | 050892 |

When you are satisfied that all the details are correct, press **ESC** to complete the entry and select Post from the options displayed at the top of the screen. When the Adjustments In screen clears press **ESC** to return to the Stock Control screen

---

**Activity 18.3**    Checking the stock details

From the Stock Control screen select Stock Details and accept the four defaults on the Stock Details screen by pressing **RETURN** . The screen will then fill with the details of the stock item that you have just entered. Notice the entries in Cost Price and In Stock.
Press **ESC** to return to the Stock Control screen.

---

**Activity 18.4**    Posting the fish purchases to stock

Having seen how to post purchases to stock you will now be able to post the two fish purchases to stock yourself. Use the following Stock Codes and Sale Prices to update the stock details and then refer to pages 38 and 39 for details of the purchases:

| Code | : | FS | |
|---|---|---|---|
| Description | : | Scallops | |
| Category | : | 2 | |
| Category Name | : | Fish | This appears automatically |
| Sale Price | : | 9.00 | |
| Cost Price | : | 0.00 | You cannot enter this |
| Unit of Sale | : | Dozen | |
| Re-Order Level | : | 50.00 | |
| Re-Order Qty | : | 200.00 | |
| Discount A% | : | 5.00 | |
| Discount B% | : | 0.00 | |
| Discount C% | : | 0.00 | |

| | | |
|---|---|---|
| Nominal Code | : | 1001 |
| Department | : | 2 |
| Tax Code | : | T0 |
| Supplier | : | HISEA |
| Location | : | Fridge |

| | | | |
|---|---|---|---|
| Code | : | FO | |
| Description | : | Oysters | |
| Category | : | 2 | |
| Category Name | : | Fish | |
| Sale Price | : | 0.35 | |
| Cost Price | : | 0.00 | You cannot enter this |
| Unit of Sale | : | Each | |
| Re-Order Level | : | 1000.00 | |
| Re-Order Qty | : | 10000.00 | |
| Discount A% | : | 5.00 | |
| Discount B% | : | 0.00 | |
| Discount C% | : | 0.00 | |

| | | |
|---|---|---|
| Nominal Code | : | 1001 |
| Department | : | 3 |
| Tax Code | : | T0 |
| Supplier | : | WILL |
| Location | : | Fridge |

Do not forget to use Adjustments In to place your purchases into stock. Refer to Task 16 for the details of the Purchase Invoices.

Finally, select Stock Details from the Stock Control screen to view the state of your strock, When you are satisfied that everything has been entered correctly press **ESC** twice to return to the Main Menu.

| Key words | Stock Control |
|---|---|
| | Update Stock Details |
| | Adjustments In |
| | Stock Details |

Task 19

# Setting up customer details

**Objective**

To learn how to post a customer's name, address and account details.

**Instructions**

Having purchased stock the company is now in a position to start selling. All sales are recorded through the Sales Ledger which is accessible from the Main Menu. As with the Purchase Ledger, before sale transactions can be posted to the ledgers the Customer Details must be recorded in the Sales Ledger. This procedure is entirely similar to the one used for Supplier Details.

---

**Activity 19.1**

Posting Customer Details into the Sales Ledger

From the Main Menu select Sales Ledger to display the Sales Ledger screen:

| | |
|---|---|
| **Customer Details** | **Address List** |
| **Batched Data Entry** | **Account Balances (Aged)** |
| **Invoice Production** | **Transaction History** |
| **Receipts** | **Day Books** |
| **Refunds** | **Statements** |
| **Contra Entries** | **Letters** |
| **Bad Debt Write Off** | |

From the Sales Ledger screen select Customer Details and enter the following information:

**Account Reference** : **JONES**

When you type in the Account Reference a prompt appears at the bottom of the screen:

**Is this a new account** : **No Yes**

It is a new account so type in **Y** for **Yes** and the highlight will move to the Account Name.

| | | |
|---|---|---|
| **Account Name** | : | **A Jones** |
| **Address** | : | **Fish Merchant** |
| | : | **38 Sole Walk** |
| | : | **Codton** |
| | : | **CO1 2DD** |
| | | |
| **Credit Limit** | : | **2000.00** |
| **Turnover** | : | **0.00** |
| | | |
| **Telephone No** | : | **0891 234567** |
| **Contact Name** | : | **Alan** |
| **Discount Code** | : | **A** |
| **Analysis Code** | : | **C1** |

You will remember that the Discount code A of 5% is recorded against stock in the Stock Control files. Allocating Discount Code A to JONES means that whenever A Jones buys from you then this discount is automatically applied to his invoice.

When you are satisfied that all the details are correct then press **ESC** to complete the entry and select Post from the list of options displayed at the bottom of the screen to post these details to the Sales Ledger.

| **Activity 19.2** | Posting further customer details to the Sales Ledger |
|---|---|

To give you some practice at posting customer details post the following to the Sales Ledger:

| Account Reference | : | SMITH |
|---|---|---|
| Account Name | : | F Smith & Son |
| Address | : | Ace Fishery |
| | : | Stall 6 |
| | : | Haddie Market |
| | : | Haddie HA3 4RT |
| | | |
| Credit Limit | : | 2000.00 |
| Turnover | : | 0.00 |
| | | |
| Telephone No | : | 0912 345678 |
| Contact Name | : | Fred |
| Discount Code | : | |
| Analysis Code | : | C2 |
| | | |
| Account Reference | : | LEE |
| Account Name | : | Lee Ling |
| Address | : | House of Peking |
| | : | 177 Canton Row |
| | : | Seatonne |
| | : | SE6 6TH |
| | | |
| Credit Limit | : | 1000.00 |
| Turnover | : | 0.00 |
| | | |
| Telephone No | : | 0834 126578 |
| Contact Name | : | Lee |
| Discount Code | : | |
| Analysis Code | : | C3 |
| | | |
| Account Reference | : | BLUE |
| Account Name | : | Blue Yonder Restaurants |

| | | |
|---|---|---|
| **Address** | : | 14 Alley Walk |
| | : | Norsea |
| | : | NO1 8EF |
| | : | |
| **Credit Limit** | : | 0.00 |
| **Turnover** | : | 0.00 |
| **Telephone No** | : | 0447 391634 |
| **Contact Name** | : | Bill |
| **Discount Code** | : | |
| **Analysis Code** | : | C4 |

| | | |
|---|---|---|
| **Account Reference** | : | OACH |
| **Account Name** | : | R Oach & P Ike |
| **Address** | : | Fish Merchants |
| | : | Humerton Wharf |
| | : | Humerton |
| | : | HU6 6YG |
| **Credit Limit** | : | 5000.00 |
| **Turnover** | : | 0.00 |
| **Telephone No** | : | 0332 875335 |
| **Contact Name** | : | Bob |
| **Discount Code** | : | A |
| **Analysis Code** | : | C5 |

| | | |
|---|---|---|
| **Account Reference** | : | CASUAL |
| **Account Name** | : | Casual Sales |
| **Address** | : | Casual |
| | : | |
| | : | |
| | : | |
| **Credit Limit** | : | 0.00 |
| **Turnover** | : | 0.00 |
| **Telephone No** | : | |
| **Contact Name** | : | |
| **Discount Code** | : | |
| **Analysis Code** | : | C6 |

Notice the amounts listed under Credit Limit. This refers to the credit your company has granted to the customer. These accounts are monthly accounts and must be settled by the fifteenth day of the month following delivery. For those customer to whom no credit has been given the terms are cash on delivery. By cash it will be understood that a cheque will suffice. We shall deal with the handling of cash later in the *Guide*.

**Activity 19.3**       Posting Opening Balances

Posting opening balances follows the same procedure used to enter purchase invoices
which you have already done in Task 15. The only difference is in the references used.
From the Sales Ledger screen select Batched Data Entry and from the Batched Data Entry
screen select Sales Invoices. Enter the following two opening balances (remember to use
**F6** to duplicate entries from the line above):

| A/C | Date | Inv | N/C | Dep | Details | Nett Amnt | Tc |
|-----|------|-----|-----|-----|---------|-----------|-----|
| JONES | 010892 | O/Bal | 9998 | 0 | Opening balance | 1321.54 | T0 |
| OACH | 010892 | O/Bal | 9998 | 0 | Opening balance | 2532.64 | T0 |

The Nominal Ledger code 9998 is called the SUSPENSE ACCOUNT and is used only for
opening balances. Notice also the Invoice reference of O/Bal which must also always be
used for opening balances.

---

**Key words**       **Discount Code**
**SUSPENSE ACCOUNT 9998**
**Opening balances**
**Invoice code O/Bal**
**Credit Limit**

| Task 20 | **Raising an invoice from stock** |
|---|---|

**Objective**

To learn how to produce an invoice from stock.

**Instructions**

During the course of the month of August the company has sold timber to a variety of customers. The maximum load sold is usually around one tonne which sells for £30. To avoid raising a large number of accounts for small amounts of money you have decided to sell your timber via the Casual Account and to lump the entire month's sales into one amount. In reality no invoices were issued for these transaction but to to follow proper accounting procedures a single invoice will be issued for the full month's sales. This will demonstrate how the invoice production procedure automatically reduces the stock level by the appropriate amount.

The invoice consists of three parts:

**Heading**

Into the Heading screen you will enter the customer details and the order number.

**Stock Items**

Into the Stock Items screen you will enter the details of the order.

**Footing**

Into the Footing screen you will enter the Tax Code, Nominal Code and Department number.

Ensure the Main Menu is on display and select the Sales Ledger.

---

**Activity 20.1**

To raise an invoice from stock

From the Sales Ledger screen select Invoice Production to display the Invoice Production screen:

> **Invoicing from Stock**
> **Credit Note Production**
> **Free Text Invoice**
> **Display Index**
> **Print Invoices**
> **Update Ledgers**
> **Delete Invoices**

From the Invoice Production screen select Invoicing from Stock and the invoice Heading screen is displayed. Enter into the Invoice Heading screen the following information:

| Invoice No. | : | 1 | This number is automatically allocated by the system |
|---|---|---|---|
| Date | : | 310892 | |
| Sales Ref. | : | CASUAL | |
| Order No. | : | 1 | |

The other items on the screen are filled in later, automatically by the system. The Total Nett, Total Tax, Total Gross and Early Payment will be filled in automatically once you have entered the Stock Items screen.

When you are satisfied that the details in the Heading screen are correct press **PgDn** or **DOWN ARROW** to move to the Stock Items screen. Enter the following information into this screen:

**Stock Code**      :     **CT**

Now press **UP ARROW** twice to make the next entry:

**Comment 1**      :     **August's timber sales**
**Quantity**         :     **22**

All the other items are filled in automatically. When you are satisfied that you have entered these details correctly press **PgDn** again to clear the details from the Stock Items screen to reveal a second, blank Stock Items screen. Now press **PgDn** again and move to the Invoice Footing screen. Press **RIGHT ARROW** followed by **UP ARROW** and enter the following information into this screen:

**Tax Code**         :     **T1**
**Nominal Code**    :     **1001**
**Dept**             :     **1**
**Description**      :     **Timber**

When these items have been entered satisfactorily press **ESC** to return to the Heading screen. Press **ESC** again and at the prompt select Save to save the details to disk. When the header screen clears press **ESC** to return to the Invoice Production screen.

---

**Activity 20.2**      To produce a hard copy of the invoice

From the Invoice Production screen select Print Invoices and into the Print Invoices screen enter the following:

| | | | |
|---|---|---|---|
| **Lower Invoice No.** | 1 | : | Press **RETURN** |
| **Upper Invoice No.** | 999999 | : | 1 |
| **Free Text Invoices** | N | : | Press **RETURN** |
| **Input File Name** | INVOICE.LYT | : | Press **RETURN** |
| **Ignore Printed Flag** | N | : | Press **RETURN** |
| **Printer or File** | P | : | Press **RETURN** |
| **Pause Between Pages** | N | : | Press **RETURN** |

The invoice will then be sent to the printer and a hard copy produced. The invoice contains the company name and address, date and account reference along with the details of the sale.

The nett price of £660.00, VAT of £115.50 and gross price of £775.50 are also shown. When the invoice has been printed press **ESC** to return to the Sales Ledger screen.

---

**Key words**        **Invoice Production**
**Raising an invoice from stock**
**Header**
**Footer**
**Stock items**

Task 21

# Entry of a sales invoice and viewing the stock

**Objective**

To learn how to post a sales order to the Sales Ledger.

**Instructions**

Having produced an invoice from stock it is now time to post the details of the sale to the ledgers. There are two ways of doing this:

(a) You can post the Sales Invoice via Batched Data Entry in the Sales Ledger and then use Adjustments Out in the Stock Control facility to reduce the stock level by the appropriate amount.

(b) You can simply update the ledgers using the Update Ledgers facility in the Invoice Production facility available in the Sales Ledger.

In this Task we shall employ the first method.

---

**Activity 21.1**

Posting a sale

From the Sales Ledger screen select Batched Data Entry and from the Batched Data entry screen select Sales Invoices. Enter the following sale (the procedure is identical to entering a purchase invoice):

| A/C | Date | Inv | N/C | Dep | Details | Nett Amnt | Tc | Tax Amnt |
|-----|------|-----|-----|-----|---------|-----------|-----|----------|
| CASUAL | 310892 | 1 | 1001 | 1 | Timber | 660.00 | T1 | 115.50 |

Note the Batch Total in the top right hand corner of the screen which now reads 775.50. When you are satisfied that you have entered the details correctly press **ESC** to complete the entry and select Post from the prompt list to post the sale to the ledgers. The posting will be:

**Credits the Debtor's Control Account** with the gross amount
**Debits the Nominal Account 1001** with the nett amount
**Debits the Tax Control Account** with the tax

When the posting is complete press **ESC** three times to return to the Main Menu.

---

**Activity 21.2**

Amending the stock

Having posted the sales order details to the Sales Ledger you will now be able to abstract the stock to supply the order.

From the Main Menu select Stock Control to display the Stock Control screen. From the Stock Control screen select Adjustments Out. Enter the following details into the Adjustments

Out screen:

| | | |
|---|---|---|
| **Stock Code** | : | **CT** |
| **Quantity** | : | **22** |
| **Cost Price** | : | **15** |
| **Narrative** | : | **August timber sale** |
| **Reference** | : | Leave blank |
| **Date** | : | **310892** |

When you are satisfied that you have entered all the details correctly, press **ESC** and at the prompt select Post to post the details to the Stock History file and the appropriate adjustment will be made to the stock. Press **ESC** to return to the Stock Control screen.

---

**Activity 21.3**

Viewing the stock

From the Stock Control screen select Stock Details and enter the following into the Stock Details screen:

| | | | |
|---|---|---|---|
| **Category or Stock Codes** | C | : | S |
| **Lower Stock Code** | 0000000000000000 | : | CT |
| **Upper Stock Code** | CT | : | CT |
| **Printer or File** | P | : | P |

Press **RETURN** when you have made sure that your printer is switched on and is On Line. The details of the company's timber stock will now be seen to consist of just 3 tonnes. This is below the re-order level so the re-order quantity must be ordered from T Feller in readiness for next month's sales. Notice that this procedure does not update the Quantity Sold Mth and YTD nor the Values Sold.

There are two other stock reports worth looking at. They are Stock History and Stock Valuation accessible form the Stock Control screen. Print out copies of both of these as well. When the printing is complete press **ESC** to return to the Main Menu.

---

**Activity 21.4**

Posting a bank receipt for a sale

All the timber sales were cash on delivery so during the course of the month you would have been paying money received for timber into the bank. These must now be recorded as a single bank receipt and posted to the ledger.

From the Main Menu select the Sales Ledger and from the Sales Ledger screen select Receipts. Post the bank receipt of £775.50 using the following details:

| | | | |
|---|---|---|---|
| **N/C Bank** | : | **1200** | Accept the default by pressing **RETURN** |

| A/C Ref. | : | CASUAL | |
|---|---|---|---|
| Payment Date | : | 310892 | |
| Cheque Number | : | | Leave blank |
| Cheque Amount | : | 775.50 | |

At this stage the Balance displays 775.50 to show that the invoice has the same outstanding value as the cheque value. At the same stage the details of the transaction are displayed and a prompt appears at the bottom of the screen:

**Method of Payment : Automatic Manual**

Select Automatic by typing in **A**. The transaction details are highlighted and the word FULL appears beneath Payment. This indicates that the account has been paid in full. Press **ESC** to indicate that your entry is complete and then select Post from the prompt to post your entry to the ledgers. When the posting is complete press **ESC** twice to return to the Main Menu.

---

**Activity 21.5**

Checking the posting

From the Main Menu select Nominal Ledger and from the Nominal Ledger screen select Control Account History. When the Control Account History screen appears select Bank Accounts to view the posting of 775.50 into the BANK CURRENT ACCOUNT.
Press **ESC** three times to return to the Main Menu.

---

**Key words**

**Posting a sale**
**Stock Details**
**Stock History**
**Stock Valuation**
**Posting a bank receipt**

## Task 22

# Raising further invoices

**Objective**

To gain practice in raising invoices from stock and posting sale details to the Sales ledger.

**Instructions**

In the previous Task it was mentioned that the details of a sale can be posted to all the appropriate ledgers using the Update Ledgers facility available within the Invoice Production facility. Ensure that the Sales Ledger screen is being displayed.

**Activity 22.1**

Updating ledgers from within Invoice Production

The following is a sale. From the Sales Ledger screen select Invoice Production and enter the following invoice into the system via Invoicing from Stock.

| | | |
|---|---|---|
| **Invoice No.** | : | **2** |
| **Date** | : | **060892** |
| **Sales Ref.** | : | **JONES** |
| **Order No.** | : | **2** |
| | | |
| **Stock Code** | : | **FS** |
| **Comment 1** | : | **Scallops** |
| **Quantity** | : | **80** |

When you enter the Quantity you will see a warning prompt:

**Balance 2041.54 > Credit Limit 2000.00**

telling you that the order is going to cause your customer to owe you more than you have officially permitted him to owe you. You decide that the excess is minimal so you ignore the warning and continue completing the invoice. Press **RETURN** twice until the highlight is over the discount of 5% and press **RETURN** again. A choice of discount options are then displayed to the right:

**Discount : A B C**

There is a highlight on A - remember that in the Stock Details discount A was set at 5%. Press **RETURN** to accept the discount into the invoice and the Discount price reads 8.55. Press **PgDn** twice and enter the following into the Footing screen:

| | | |
|---|---|---|
| **Tax Code** | : | **T0** |
| **Nominal Account Code** | : | **1001** |
| **Department** | : | **2** |
| **Description** | : | **Scallops** |

When you have entered these details press **ESC** twice and Save the invoice to disk for printing at a later time. When the saving is complete press **ESC** again to return to the Invoice Production screen.

From the Invoice Production screen select Update Ledgers and enter the following information into the Update Ledgers screen:

| | | |
|---|---|---|
| **Lower Invoice No.** | 1 : | 2 |
| **Upper Invoice No .** | 2 : | Press **RETURN** |
| **Printer or File** | P : | Press **RETURN** |

**Switch the Printer On and Press RETURN**

Do this and the ledgers will all be automatically updated by the system as will the Stock Control details and a report will be printed giving a one line description of the invoice details.

When this is complete press **ESC** to return to the Sales Ledger screen.

---

**Activity 22.2**

Checking the Sales Invoices display

From the Sales Ledger screen select Transaction History and on the Transaction History screen enter the Lower and Upper Account References as JONES. When the Transaction History screen is displayed you will see the details of the two transactions in the JONES account, namely the Opening balance and this last sale. The asterisk at the side of the Value indicates an unpaid transaction.

Press **ESC** twice to return to the Main Menu.

---

**Activity 22.3**

Checking the Nominal Ledger display

From the Main Menu select the Nominal Ledger and from the Nominal Ledger screen select Transaction History and on the Transaction History screen enter the Lower and Upper Account References as 1001. When the Transaction History screen is displayed you will see the history of the Nominal Account code 1001 called STOCK. The last transaction entered is the sale to JONES.

Press **ESC** twice to return to the Main Menu.

---

**Activity 22.4**

Checking the Stock Details display

From the Main Menu select Stock Control and from the Stock Control screen select Stock Details. Accept the four default values in the first Stock Details screen and when the third Stock Details screen is displayed you will see the stock of scallops has been decreased by the appropriate amount and you now have 170 dozen in stock. Notice, also, that because you chose the Update Ledgers option the Quantity and Value Sold Mth and YTD,

along with the date of the last sale have been recorded.
Press ESC twice to return to the Main Menu.

---

**Activity 22.5**    Raising further invoices

To familiarise yourself with the manipulations involved in the raising of invoices and the updating of the ledgers enter the following two sales invoices into the system:

| | | |
|---|---|---|
| **Invoice No.** | : | **3** |
| **Date** | : | **110892** |
| **Sales Ref.** | : | **OACH** |
| **Order No.** | : | **3** |

This sale involves two items. Enter the first item into the Stock Items screen and when that entry is complete press PgDn to reveal an empty Stock Items screen. Enter the second item into this screen.

| | | |
|---|---|---|
| **Stock Code** | : | **FO** |
| **Comment 1** | : | **Oysters** |
| **Quantity** | : | **2000.00** |

| | | |
|---|---|---|
| **Stock Code** | : | **FS** |
| **Comment 1** | : | **Scallops** |
| **Quantity** | : | **50.00** |

Leave the other items with their default values and enter the following into the Footing screen:

| | | |
|---|---|---|
| **Tax Code** | : | **TO** |
| **Nominal Account Code** | : | **1001** |
| **Department** | : | **4**   Department 4 refers to mixed sales of scallops and oysters |
| **Description** | : | **Scallops & Oysters** |

| | | |
|---|---|---|
| **Invoice No** | : | **4** |
| **Date** | : | **200892** |
| **Sales Ref.** | : | **LEE** |
| **Order No.** | : | **4** |

| | | |
|---|---|---|
| **Stock Code** | : | **FO** |
| **Comment** | : | **Oysters** |
| **Quantity** | : | **5000.00** |

When you enter the Quantity figure of 5000 a warning appears to the right:

**Balance 1750.00 > Credit Limit 1000.00**

You decide that this balance is too excessive. Move the highlight back to Quantity and amend the entry to 2500.00 by overtyping. The warning message disappears. To compensate Lee Ling you decide to give him a 5% discount. When the highlight is opposite Discount % press **RETURN**. The options of discounts A, B or C appear with a highlight on the A. Press **RETURN** to select this discount and the Discount price now reads 0.33.

Enter the following into the Footing screen:

| | | |
|---|---|---|
| **Tax Code** | : | **T0** |
| **Nominal Account Code** | : | **1001** |
| **Department** | : | **3** |
| **Desacription** | : | **Oysters** |

When you have entered all the details of both invoices press **ESC** to return to the Invoice Production screen and select Print Invoices and print all outstanding invoices.

---

**Activity 22.6**

Update the ledgers

Now you have raised and printed the two invoices select Update Ledgers from the Invoice Production screen to update all the necessary ledgers automatically with the details of invoices 3 and 4.

---

**Activity 22.7**

Changing a customer's details

You have agreed to Lee Ling's request to increase his credit limit because of his prompt payment and past payment record. Display the Sales Ledger screen and select Customer Details.

Alongside Account Reference enter the code **LEE** and press **RETURN**. The LEE account details appear. Move the highlight down to Credit Limit and type in **2000** to increase his limit. Notice that the Turnover now reads 831.25, the value of his last purchase.

Press **ESC** and select Post from the prompt to post the details to the ledger. When the posting is complete press **ESC** to return to the Sales Ledger screen.

---

**Activity 22.8**

The sale to LEE was less than his order so he paid promptly and requested his credit limit be increased. His payment of £831.25 is now in the bank. Post this transaction as a sale receipt. Select Receipts from the Sales Ledger screen and use the details contained in the invoice report issued in Activity 22.5.

| Key words | **Raising invoices** |
| --- | --- |
| | **Posting sales** |

Task 23 **Issuing a statement**

**Objective**    To learn how to issue a statement follow the stock delivery to a customer.

**Instruction**   A statement to a customer shows all outstanding payments due. It may also contain a message to the customer telling them, for example, when you expect to receive payment. It is customary practice to send a statement to all credit customers who have outstanding payments to make.

---

**Activity 23.1**     Issuing a Statement

From the Sales Ledger screen select Statements and enter the following into the Statements screen:

| | | |
|---|---|---|
| **Lower Accounts Reference** | : | **JONES** |
| **Upper Accounts Reference** | : | **JONES** |
| **Enter Date of report** | : | **310892** |

Give this as the end of the month. The only items that will appear on the statement are those transactions that are dated up to this date.

| | | |
|---|---|---|
| **Printer or File** | : | **P** |
| **Print Individual Items** | : | **Y** |
| **Address on Statement** | : | **Y** |
| **Message Line 1** | : | _____ |
| **Message Line 2** | : | **CREDIT LIMIT EXCEEDED** |
| **Message Line 3** | : | _____ |

The required statement will now be issued at the printer.

---

**Activity 23.2**     Issuing a further statement

Your company has a second customer with outstanding credit, namely R Oach and P Ike. Produce a statement for the customer using the Account Reference OACH.

---

**Key words**     **Statement**
**Statement Date**

# Section C: Order Processing

The Financial Controller component of the Sage Sterling Accounting system provides a measure of automated accounting that is not available in the other components. In this Section you will learn how to manipulate the Sales and Purchase Order Processing features of the Financial Controller.

In Sections A and B you learnt how to enter the details of sales and purchases into the Sales and Purchase Ledgers, how to raise an invoice from stock based on the details of the sale and how to raise a statement for ownward transmission to a customer and a remittance advice for onward transmisison to a supplier. Many of these manipulations of the system duplicated earlier manipulations and in the Sales and Purchase Order Processing facility such duplicated manipulations are done automatically.

The following table describes which of the Tasks in this Section are available in which component of the Sage Sterling Accounting system:

| Task | 24 | 25 | 26 | 27 | 28 | 29 |
|------|----|----|----|----|----|----|
| Bookkeeper | no | no | no | no | no | no |
| Accountant | no | no | no | no | no | no |
| Accountant + | no | no | no | no | no | no |
| Financial Controller | yes | yes | yes | yes | yes | yes |

# Task 24    **Entering a sales order**

**Objective**      To learn how to enter orders into the Sales Order Processing facility.

**Instructions**   One of the automatic features of the Sales Order Processing facility is that it automatically transfers details of a sales order onto an invoice. As a consequence the screen associated with the entry of a Sales Order is very similar to that used for the production of an Invoice from Stock. If you refer to Task 20 as you work your way through this Task you will see the similarity. From the Main Menu select the Sales Order Processing option to display the Sales Order Processing screen:

> **Enter Sales Orders**
> **Process Sales Orders**
> **Enquiries**
> **Order Status Reports**
> **Order Acknowledgement**
> **Amend Despatches**
> **Create Invoice Details**
> **Delete Orders**

Just as with invoice production there are three parts to the Sales Order, the Heading, the Stock Items and the Footing. The completion of each part will be a separate activity. From the Sales Order Processing screen select Enter Sales Orders to display the Enter Sales Orders screeen.

---

**Activity 24.1**    Filling in the Sales Order Header screen

The screen display you now see before you is the Header display of the Sales Order entry system. Enter the following details into this screen:

| | | | |
|---|---|---|---|
| **Order No.** | : | **5** | This is entered automatically |
| **Date** | : | **140892** | |
| **Sales Ref.** | : | **SMITH** | |
| **Customer Name** | : | **F Smith & Son** | |
| **Customer Address** | : | **Ace Fishery** | |
| | : | **Stall 6** | |
| | : | **Haddie Market** | |
| | : | **Haddie HA3 4RT** | |
| | | | |
| **Telephone** | : | **0912 345678** | |
| **Delivery Name** | : | —— **AS INVOICED** —— | |
| **Delivery Address** | : | | |
| | : | | |
| | : | | |
| | : | | |

---

| | | | |
|---|---|---|---|
| **Order Taken By** | : | **Self** | |
| **Invoice No.** | : | **0** | This is automatically filled when the invoice is produced |
| **Due Delivery** | : | **160892** | |
| **Customer Order No.** | : | | Leave blank |

This completes the Header screen as far as your entry is concerned. The remaining six items cannot be filled in by you, they are done automatically by the system.

When you are satisfied that the Header screen has been correctly entered press **PgDn** to move to the Stock Item screen.

---

**Activity 24.2**

Filling in the Sales Order Stock Items screen

Enter the following details into the Stock Items screen:

**Stock Code** : **FO**

**Quantity** : **3000**

For all the other details on this screen accept the default as displayed. When you are satisfied that this screen has been correctly completed press **PgDn** to clear the details from the screen. Now enter the next stock item:

**Stock Code** : **FS**

**Quantity** : **50**

Again, leave all other details as the default and press **PgDn** to complete your entry to reveal a second, blank Stock Items screen. As this is the last stock for the order press **PgDn** again to reveal the Footing screen.

---

**Activity 24.3**

Filling in the Sales Order Footing screen

Take a close look at the contents of the Footing screen. The only items to be entered here by you are:

**Tax Code** : **T0**
**Nominal Code** : **1001**
**Department** : **4**

When you are satisfied that all the details are correct press **ESC** to return to the Header screen. Now press **ESC** again to complete the Sales Order Entry and select Post from the displayed prompt to post the details of this Sales Order to the Sales and Nominal Ledgers.

**Activity 24.4**     Entering a further Sales Order

Lee Ling of The House of Peking has just rung through an order for 80 dozen scallops. Using the Account Reference code LEE for Lee Ling, FS for scallops, Tax Code TO, Nominal code 1001 and Department 2, enter this order into the Sales Order Processing system with the Date 210892.

**Key words**     **Entering a Sales Order**
**Header screen**
**Stock Items screen**
**Footer screen**

## Task 25 — Allocating stock to an order

**Objectives:** To learn how stock is allocated to orders within the Sales Order Processing facility.

**Instructions** When a Sales Order has first been entered into the system it is rated as a Back Order. All Back Orders require to have the appropriate stock allocated to them from the Stock Control facility. Once this has been done the order is rated as an Outstanding Order - outstanding in the sense that it is still a live order but has not yet been despatched. From the Sales Order Processing screen Process Sales orders and on the Process Sales Orders screen you will see displayed the two Sales Orders you have just entered.

---

**Activity 25.1**

At the bottom of the Process Sales Orders screen you will see the prompt:

**Do you want to : Allocate Despatch**

Select Allocate and at the prompt:

**Method of Processing : Automatic Manual**

select Automatic. When this process is complete press **ESC** to return to the Process Sales Orders screen where you will see that the Allocate column displays FULL for the order placed by SMITH to signify that there was sufficient stock available to fully allocate stock to this order. The stock allocated to this order will have been automatically subtracted from the stock held. The order placed by LEE has the annotation PART in the Allocate column to indicate that there were insufficient scallops in stock to completely fill the order. This order remains a Back Order until there is sufficient stock to fill it.

---

**Activity 25.2**

Attempting to despatch an order

At the bottom of the Process Sales Orders screen is the prompt:

**Do you want to : Allocate Despatch**

Select Despatch and the screen displays the message:

**No invoice has been produced for this order**

The system will not let you despatch an order until you have produced an invoice for it.

Task 26

# Producing the paperwork to accompany a sale

**Objectives**

To learn how to produce all the necessary documentation that is associated with the despatch of goods.

**Instructions**

The Sales Order to SMITH has been fully allocated from stock and is now an Outstanding Order that requires to be despatched.

---

**Activity 26.1**

Checking Outstanding Orders

From the Main Menu select Sales Order Processing and from the Sales Order Processing screen select Enquiries. At each question on the Enquiries screen press **RETURN** to accept the default response to display the two sales orders that have been entered into the system.

When you are satisfied that the SMITH order is ready for despatch press **ESC** to return to the Sales Order Processing screen. From this screen select Process Sales Orders.

---

**Activity 26.2**

Printing the Order Sheets

From the Process Sales Order screen select Order Sheets and enter all the details necessary to print out the Outstanding Orders. This will cause the SMITH order details to be sent to the printer and a hard copy produced.

---

**Activity 26.3**

Creating an invoice

Ensure that the Sales Order Processing screen is being displayed and select Create Invoice Details. Enter the order number range as 5 to 6 and a report will be produced showing various details of the order including the invoice number that has been allocated to this transaction.

The invoice for the SMITH order has now been produced and all appropriate ledgers updated. We could now proceed to despatch the order but before we do this we shall print out the invoice for delivery along with the order.

Press **ESC** until the Main Menu is displayed.

**Activity 26.4**　Printing the invoice and despatch note

From the Main Menu select Sales Ledger and from the Sales Ledger screen select Invoice Production and print both an invoice and a despatch note for the SMITH order.

---

**Key words**　　**Enquiries**
**Order Sheets**
**Create Invoices**
**Invoice Production**
**Despatch Note**

# Despatching an order and updating the ledgers

**Objectives:**

To learn how to use the Sales Order Processing facility to complete an order.

**Instructions**

Having entered a sales order into the system and having allocated stock to it and produced all the necessary paperwork to accompany the order we must now despatch the order. Here the accounting procedure follows the physical procedure. The despatch process completes the allocation of stock to the order by adding the stock to the order and subtracting it from the stock held.

Ensure that the Main Menu is being displayed and select Sales Order Processing. From the Sales Order Processing screen select Process Sales Orders to display the two orders currently in the system.

---

**Activity 27.1**

To despatch an order

Place the highlight over the SMITH order and at the prompt at the bottom of the screen:

**Do you want to    :    Allocate    Despatch**

Select Despatch. The system then automatically transfers stock from the stock file to the order. The FULL message in the Allocate column disappears and in the despatch column the word COMPLETE appears to indicate that the order has been despatch.

When you are satisfied that the order is completely despatched press **ESC** until you return to the Main Menu.

---

**Activity 27.2**

To complete an order by Updating the ledgers

From the Main Menu select Sales Ledger and from the Sales Ledger screen select Invoice Production. From the Invoice Production screen select Update Ledgers and press **RETURN** to accept the defaults to each prompt. The Nominal Ledger will then be automatically updated and a report sent to the printer. When the report has been printed you will be returned to the Invoice Production menu.

Press **ESC** twice to return you to the Main Menu.

**Activity 27.3**    Checking the stock levels

From the Main Menu select Stock Control and follow the procedure in Task 21 to obtain information about the current state of the stock held. You will see that the Oysters and Scallops have been reduced by the amount necessary to fulfill the SMITH order but nothing has been subtracted for the LEE order. This will not happen until we either despatch the PART order or obtain sufficient supplies to fill the order and then despatch the FULL order.

**Key words**    **Despatch an order**
                 **Update Ledgers**

Task 28          **Viewing the stock**

**Objective**       To review the stock viewing facility.

**Instructions**    Having made a number of sales you need to know how much stock you have left to
                    discover whether you need to purchase more to enable you to make further sales.

---

**Activity 28.1**       Viewing the stock

From the Main Menu select Stock Control and from the Stock Control screen select Stock
Details. You will be confronted by the timber stock details from which you will see that you
only have 3 tonnes left. This is below the re-order level of 5 tonnes so you make a note to
place an order with T Feller for another 25 tonnes of cut timber.

Press **RETURN** and you will see the oyster stock on display. You only have 2500
oysters left and you decide to hold off from purchasing any more for the moment as this
figure is larger than the re-order level of 1000 oysters.

Press **RETURN** again to view the scallops stock. You only have 70 dozen in stock.
This is above the re-order level but you have just failed to complete a Sales Order for the
LEE account who wants 80 dozen so you decide to re-order the re-order quantity of 200
dozen. This you will do in the next Task.

Press **ESC** twice to return to the Main Menu.

---

**Key words**       **Viewing the stock**

# Processing a purchase order

**Objective**    To learn how to use the Purchase Order Processing facility.

**Instructions**    The Sales Order Processing facility still contains a PART allocated order to Lee Ling. We could create an invoice and despatch this order as a part order if we so wish but instead we shall order more stock to enable us to complete the order using the Purchase Order Processing facility of the Financial Manager.

The Purchase Order Processing facility operates in just the same way as the Sales Order Processing with the three differences being:

Account references are to suppliers
An order can have a status of one of the following:

**On-Order**
**Cancelled**
**Part Delivered**
**Complete**

The Accounts ledgers are not updated.

When an entered purchase order is given the status of Complete then the Stock Quantity that the order contains is automatically transferred to stock. You will then have to enter the purchase invoice details and any payment you make against the invoice using the usual procedures.

---

**Activity 29.1**    Entering a Purchase Order

From the Main Menu select Purchase Order Processing to display the Purchase Order Processing screen:

**Enter Purchase Orders**
**Process Purchase Orders**
**Enquiries**
**Order Status Reports**
**Order Document**
**Amend Deliveries**
**Delete Orders**

Select Enter Purchase Orders and enter and post the following two purchase orders into the Enter Purchase Order screens:

**100 dozen scallops from HISEA @ £6.00, dated 210892**

**100 dozen scallops from SMILE @ £5.75, dated 220892**

---

**Activity 29.2**    Processing a purchase order

From the Purchase Order Processing screen select Process Purchase Orders and process the two orders that you have just enterd in the previous Activity. Just as with Sales Orders you will have to Allocate and then Despatch the order so as to give it the status of Complete.

When you have completed this process return to the Main Menu and select Stock Control. From the Stock Control screen select Stock Details and see for yourself that the stock has been posted.

---

**Activity 29.3**    Posting the Purchase Invoice

During the Purchase Order Processing the stock was automatically updated but the account ledgers were not. These cannot be updated until the Purchase Invoice arrives from your supplier - it will contain details of which you are unaware, such as Invoice number, for example.

Both invoices have now arrived and so now they must be posted to the ledgers using the additional information:

**HISEA Invoice number is 3235**

**SMILE Invoice number is 106**

Both invoices relate to Noimal Code 1001 for stock, Department number 2 and carry a zero rate of VAT

---

**Activity 29.4**    Posting a purchase invoice payment

You have no credit arrangements with the SMILE account so the delivery was paid for COD with cheque number 4. Post this payment into the ledgers.

---

**Activity 29.5**    Completing a Sales Order

A Back-Order still exists from the previous Task. The sales order for the LEE account could not be fully allocated. Return to the Sales Order Processing facility and complete the order by allocating stock to it and despatching it.

# Section D: Ending the month's accounting ■■■■

You have completed your first month's trading since your expansion and now is the time to reconcile all your accounts for the month. In this Section you will learn how to produce all the necessary month-end reports and how to complete the month's accounting.

The following table describes which of the Tasks in this Section are available in which component of the Sage Sterling Accounting system:

| Task | 30 | 31 | 32 | 33 | 34 | 35 | 36 | 37 | 38 | 39 | 40 | 41 |
|------|----|----|----|----|----|----|----|----|----|----|----|----|
| Bookkeeper | yes | yes | no | no | yes | yes | yes | no | no | yes | yes | yes |
| Accountant | yes | yes | yes | no | yes | yes | yes | yes | yes | yes | yes | yes |
| Accountant + | yes | yes | yes | yes | yes | yes | yes | yes | yes | yes | yes | yes |
| Financial Controller | yes | yes | yes | yes | yes | yes | yes | yes | yes | yes | yes | yes |

Task 30

# Completing the first month's trading

**Objective**    To reinforce and test the ability to post sale transactions.

**Instructions**    By way of a review you will now be required to post sale and purchase transactions to the appropriate ledgers using the Sales and Purchase Order Processing facilities.

---

**Activity 30.1**    Processing Purchase Orders

As the month has progressed you have found trade to be quite brisk. As a consequence you have had to make a number of further purchases to satisfy your customer's needs. The following are the details of the purchase orders to be entered into the system

**50 dozen scallops at £6.00 per dozen from HISEA delivered with invoice number 3240, dated 230892**

**100 dozen scallops at £5.45 per dozen from SMILE delivered with invoice number 109, dated 230892 and paid for COD with cheque number 5**

**3000 oysters at 25p each from WILL delivered with invoice number 2802, dated 240892 and paid for COD with cheque number 6**

**2000 oysters from at 27p each from ABC delivered with invoice number 301, dated 250892**

**25 tonnes timber from WOOD at £15 per tonne delivered with invoice number 136, dated 280892**

They all relate to Nominal Code 1001 for stock and, except for the timber, they are all zero rated for VAT.
From the Main Menu select Purchase Order Processing and enter and process these purchase invoices and the payments made for COD.

---

**Activity 30.2**    Processing Sales Orders

To match the purchasing activity a number of sales have been made. The details of the sales are as follows:

**125 scallops to BLUE despatched 230892 paid for COD**

**10 scallops to JONES despatched 240892**

The JONES order exceeds his Credit Limit by 95.54 but let the order go through.

**125 scallops and 100 oysters to OACH despatched 290892**

**1500 oysters to LEE despatched 300892**

From the Main Menu select Sales Order Processing and enter and process these sales invoices.

| Key words | Sales and Purchase Order Processing |
|---|---|

Task 31       **Monthly procedures**

**Objective**    To review the standard reporting facilities that are available within the system.

**Instructions**  Throughout the course of a month's accounting it may be desired to obtain detailed information regarding the state of the accounts. Here we shall review those standard reporting facilities that we have not so far discussed. Whilst it is possible to view all of these reports on the screen you will attain a far clearer view of the state of affairs if you produce a printed copy for each report.

---

**Activity 31.1**    Viewing the Quick Ratio report

The Quick Ratio report gives a list of your current liquidity. It can list the current balance of your bank account, money owing to creditors and money owed by debtors.

From the Main Menu select Nominal Ledger and from the Nominal Ledger screen select Quick Ratio. At the prompt:

### Do you wish to : View Edit

select Edit and the Quick Ratio screen will be displayed with no entries in it. Enter the following Nominal Account codes:

| | |
|---|---|
| 1200 | **BANK CURRENT ACCOUNT** |
| 2100 | **CREDITORS CONTROL ACCOUNT** |
| 1100 | **DEBTORS CONTROL ACCOUNT** |
| 1001 | **STOCK** |

When you are satisfied that you have entered everything press **ESC** and return to the Nominal Ledger display. From the Nominal Ledger display re-select Quick Ratio and this time elect to View it. Note that only 12 accounts can be displayed in any one Quick Ratio report.

| N/C | Account Name | Debit | Credit |
|---|---|---|---|
| 1200 | **BANK CURRENT ACCOUNT** | 3731.75 | |
| 2100 | **CREDITORS CONTROL ACCOUNT** | | 4831.90 |
| 1100 | **DEBTORS CONTROL ACCOUNT** | 9683.18 | |
| 1001 | **STOCK** | | 385.25 |
| | | **8197.78** | |

This is showing that the cash you have in the bank is not sufficient to pay your creditors. However, your debtors owe you a substantial sum and if you can get some of that paid in then you could easily settle your debts. You also have a reasonable amount of money tied up in stock.

Press **ESC** to return to the Nominal Ledger screen.

---

**Activity 31.2**  Viewing the Address List

There will undoubtedly be times when you wish to have sight of your customer or supplier list. The customer list can be viewed from the Sales Ledger option on the Main Menu. From the Sales Ledger screen select Address List. Press **RETURN** to accept the default Lower and Upper Account References and select A in response to:

### Name or Address:

The list of names and addresses of your customers will then appear on the screen, four at a time. Press **RETURN** to view more.

Repeat this procedure by restricting the display to Names only and now you see there is room to display all six, two to a line.

The same procedure is available from within the Purchase Ledger to view the names and address of your suppliers. Press **ESC** twice to return to the Main Menu and select Purchase Ledger. From the Purchase Ledger display select Address List and view the list of suppliers.

---

**Key words**  **Standard reports**
**Quick Ratio**
**Address List**

Task 32                    **Ending the month**

**Objective**              To learn how to complete a month's accounting.

**Instructions**           When the accounting month comes to an end all the ledgers must be balanced and
                           reconciled with each other. This means, amongst other things, that all the Prepayments and
                           Accruals must be posted, all the Recurring Entries must be posted, all the Asset Deprecia-
                           tions must be posted and the Stock adjusted so that the following month's stock system
                           commences with Quantity Sold and Value Sold this Month set at zero. Fortunately, all these
                           procedures are performed automatically by the Sage Sterling Accounting system via the
                           Utilities option on the Main Menu.
                               Ensure that the Main Menu is being displayed and select Utilities:

                               **Audit Trail**
                               **Departments**
                               **VAT Code Changes**
                               **Month End**
                               **Year End**
                               **Data File Utilities**
                               **Backup Utilities**

                           From the Utilities screen select Month End to display the Month End screen:

                               **Recurring Entries**
                               **Prepayments & Accruals**
                               **Depreciation**
                               **Stock**

                           When you posted Recurring Entries, Prepayments & Accruals and Depreciation earlier in the
                           *Guide* it was mentioned that these monthly items are not posted automatically. Instead their
                           posting into the ledgers hads to be initiated by you. This is where you do that.

---

**Activity 32.1**         Posting the month's Recurring Entries

                          From the Month End screen select Recurring Entries and the following message is  dis-
                          played:

                          **This routine will post all the transactions specified in the
                          list of recurring transactions as new transactions on the
                          existing Audit Trail. Transactions with dates will be posted
                          with the given date as the transaction date. Transactions with
                          TODAY in the date field will be posted with the system date as
                          the transaction date.**

                          **Press ESC to finish, RETURN to continue**

                          Press **RETURN** to permit the system to post the recurring entries to the Nominal Ledger to
                          produce a report that can be sent to either a file or the printer. Elect to have the report sent to

the printer so that you can see what has been posted.

Notice that the system does not prevent you from running this option more than once per month, thereby re-posting the Recurring Entries.

When the posting is complete you are returned to the Month End screen.

---

**Activity 32.2**   Posting the month's Prepayments and Accruals

From the Month End screen select Prepayments and Accruals and the following message is displayed:

**This routine will post Journal Debits to the individual Nominal Accounts associated with each prepayment or accrual and Journal Credits to each Prepayment or Accrual Account. Reverse Journals for the total amount will also be posted for prepayment in their first month and accruals in their last month. The individual Nominal Accounts should appear in the Profit & Loss Report. The Prepayment and Accruals should appear in the Balance Sheet.**

**Press ESC to finish, RETURN to continue**

Press **RETURN** to permit the system to post the prepayments and accruals entries to the Nominal Ledger and produce a report that can be sent to either a file or the printer. Elect to have the report sent to the printer so that you can see what has been posted.

Notice that the system does not prevent you from running this option more than once per month, thereby re-posting the Prepayments and Accruals.

When the posting is complete you are returned to the Month End screen.

---

**Activity 32.3**   Posting the month's Depreciation

From the Month End screen select Depreciation and the following message is displayed:

**This routine will post Journal Credits to the individual Accumulated Depreciation Accounts associated with each fixed asset and a single balancing Journal Debit to the Depreciation Expense Account. The Accumulated Depreciation Accounts should appear under Fixed Assets in the Balance Sheet. The Depreciation Expense Account should appear in the Profit & Loss Report**

**Press ESC to finish, RETURN to continue**

Press **RETURN** to permit the system to post the depreciation entries to the Nominal Ledger and produce a report that can be sent to either a file or the printer. Elect to have the report sent to the printer so that you can see what has been posted.

Notice that the system does not prevent you from running this option more than once per month, thereby re-posting the Depreciations.

When the posting is complete you are returned to the Month End screen. Press **ESC** twice to return to the Main Menu.

---

**Activity 32.4**

To check the postings

From the Main Menu select the Nominal Ledger. From the Nominal Ledger screen select Asset Valuation and display the report on the screen. You will notice that the appropriate adjustments to the asset values have been posted and that a star has been entered beneath the P. This star indicates that the month's depreciation has been posted.

When you are satisfied that you appreciate the Asset Valuation screen press **ESC** to return to the Nominal Ledger screen.

From the Nominal Ledger screen select

**Prepayments and Accruals**
**Recurring Entries**
**Depreciation**

in turn and view the effects of the postings there.

---

**Key words**

**Month End procedures**
**Recurring Entries**
**Prepayments and Accruals**
**Depreciation**
**Stock Month End**

# Stock reports

**Objectives**

To learn how to obtain a stock reports and how to re-set the stock levels at the end of an accounting month in readiness for the next month's trading.

**Instructions**

From the Main Menu select Stock Control to display the various options that are available from the Stock Control screen:

> **Update Stock Details**
> **Categories**
> **Adjustments In**
> **Adjustments Out**
> **Stock Transfer**
> **Stock Details**
> **Stock History**
> **Stock Valuation**
> **Stock Profit**
> **Stock Explosion**
> **Re-Order Levels**

---

**Activity 33.1**

Viewing the Stock Reports

Various Stock Reports are available via the Stock Control option on the Main Menu. From the Main Menu select Stock Control and view each of the stock reports offered:

**Stock History**
This report displays all the stock movements for each stock item in the report.
     Accept the four defaults on the Stock History screen and the first history is that of the Timber . Note the three transactions consist of two deliveries and one sale.

**Stock Valuation**
This report lists the quantities, values and anticipated monthly sales of each item in stock. The Stock Valuation report is best printed as it is too wide and detailed to view easily on the screen. You will find your timber is valued at £420.00 and your fish at £1951.00.

**Profit Report**
This report lists the profit and percentage profit of each item that has sold either during the Month or during the Year to Date.  The profit on your timber was £330 and on your fish £2426.25.

**Re-order level report**
The Re-order Levels report will display details of all  those stock items that have fallen on or below the recorded re-order level. The re-order quantity is also displayed.

---

**Activity 33.2**    Re-setting the stock month to-date values

From the Month End screen select Stock and the following message is displayed:

**WARNING**

**This routine will automatically zero the QUANTITY
SOLD and SALES VALUE in the stock item for the
current period ONLY!**

**Please ensure the following reports have been
printed before proceeding with this routine.**

**STOCK HISTORY REPORT
STOCK VALUATION REPORT
STOCK PROFIT REPORT**

**Press ESC to finish, RETURN to continue.**

Press **RETURN** to permit the system to re-set the month to-date stock values.
     When the posting is complete you are automatically returned to the Month End screen.
Press **ESC** twice to return to the Main Menu.

---

**Activity 33.3**    To check the postings

From the Main Menu select Stock Control and from the Stock Control screen select Stock
Details where you will see that the Quantity Sold Mth and Value Sold Mth fields have
indeed been set at zero.

---

**Key words**    **Stock History
Stock Valuation
Profit Report
Re-Order Level Report
Re-setting stock month to-date values**

Task 34            **The Sales Ledger accounts balances**

**Objective**         To produce a report that lists all the month's sales accounts that have produced a turnover
during the last month.

**Instructions**      From the Main Menu select the Sales Ledger and from the Sales Ledger screen select
Account Balanced (Aged), where Aged refers to balances up to a specified date.

---

**Activity 34.1**     Displaying the complete sales turnover analysis

On the Account Balances screen enter the following:

| | | |
|---|---|---|
| **Lower Account Reference** | : | **BLUE** |
| **Upper Account Reference** | : | **SMITH** |
| **Date** | : | **310892** |
| **Display, Print or File** | : | **D** |

After a few moments you will see all the sales transactions for which there is an outstanding
payment due for the month of August listed on the screen. There are four of them:

**JONES at    2095.54**
**LEE at       1245.00**
**OACH at     4842.64**
**SMITH at    1500.00**

Press **ESC** to return to the Sales Ledger screen.

---

**Activity 34.2**     Displaying a restricted set of sales accounts

By entering different Account References and Date you will be able to produce a restricted
report. Enter the Lower Account Reference as JONES and the Upper Account Reference as
OACH. The display will now be restricted to three sales accounts as you will see.
     When you are satisfied that you appreciate this report press **ESC** to return to the Sales
Ledger screen. Now repeat the Activity, only this time produce a printout. When your
printout is complete you will be returned automatically to the Purchase Ledger screen.
     Press **ESC** to return to the Main Menu.

---

**Key words**         **Account Balances (Aged)**

Task 35      **The Purchase Ledger accounts balances**

**Objective**      To produce a report that lists all the month's purchase accounts that have produced a turnover during the last month.

**Instructions**      From the Main Menu select the Purchase Ledger and from the Purchase Ledger screen select Account Balances (Aged).

---

**Activity 35.1**      Displaying the complete purchase turnover analysis

On the Account Balances screen enter the following:

| | | |
|---|---|---|
| **Lower Account Reference** | : | **ABC** |
| **Upper Account Reference** | : | **WOOD** |
| **Date** | : | **310892** |
| **Display, Print or File** | : | **D** |

After a few moments you will see all the purchase transactions for which you are indebted for the month of August listed on the screen. There are three of them:

| | |
|---|---|
| **ABC at** | **540.00** |
| **HISEA at** | **3254.79** |
| **WOOD at** | **1037.11** |

Press **ESC** to return to the Purchase Ledger screen.

---

**Activity 35.2**      Displaying a restricted set of purchase accounts

By entering different Account References and Date you will be able to produce a restricted report. Enter the Lower Account Reference as WOOD and the Upper Account Reference as WOOD. The display will now be restricted to one purchase account only as you will see.
     When you are satisfied that you appreciate this report press **ESC** to return to the Purchase Ledger screen. Now repeat the Activity, only this time produce a printout.
     When your printout is complete you will be returned automatically to the Purchase Ledger screen. Press **ESC** to return to the Main Menu.

---

**Key words**      **Account Balances (Aged)**

## Task 36     **The Audit Trail**

**Objective**

To appreciate the information content of the Audit Trail.

**Instructions**

The most important report of any accounting system is the Audit Trail which lists the details of every single transaction recorded in the system. In the Sage Sterling Accounting System the Audit Trail is accessed via the Utilities option on the Main Menu.

---

**Activity 36.1**

Accessing the Audit Trail

Ensure that the Main Menu is being displayed and select the Utilities option. From the Utilities screen select Audit Trail and accept the three default options to display the Audit Trail screen. Amongst the information on the Audit Trail are the items:

**No.**     The transaction number. The transactions are listed in the order in which they were entered into the system.

**Tp**     This refers to Type of transaction, for example, BR refers to a Bank Receipt and JD refers to a Journal Debit.

The remainder of the items are self explanatory. At the bottom of the screen is a message:

**Press ESC to finish, RETURN to continue, RIGHT ARROW for Payment Details**

Press **RIGHT ARROW** and the last three colums on the right hand side of the screen, under the heading Invoice Details, change to four columns describing Payment Details. Again the items listed are self-explantory.

As you will appreciate, reading the Audit Trail each item describes the point of entry of each posting into the system and its eventual location in the Nominal Ledger. For example, the first Audit Trail entry is the Bank Receipt of the Formation capital. Here the transaction was recorded as a debit into the BANK CURRENT ACCOUNT in the Bank Control Account number 1200. This was then automatically entered as a credit in the Nominal Account 3102 - STARTUP CAPITAL.

Only twelve transactions can be viewed at a time. Press **RETURN** to display the next twelve. At the very end of the list you will notice the transactions related to recurring entries, repayments and depreciation.

Press **ESC** twice to return to the Main Menu.

---

**Activity 36.2**

Obtaining a hard copy of the Audit Trail

Re-enter the Audit Trail option of the Utilities and this time send the Audit Trail to the printer. From the printout you will see the Payment Details included on the same line as the Invoice Details.

**Key words**   **Audit Trail**
                 **Transaction type Tp**

Task 37          **The Report Generator**

**Objective**          To learn how to generate bespoke reports.

**Instructions**          From the Main Menu select Report Generator to display the Report Generator screen:

> **Sales Ledger**
> **Purchase Ledger**
> **Nominal Ledger**
> **Management Reports**
> **Invoice Production**
> **Stock Control**
> **Sales Order Processing**
> **Purchase Order Processing**

From the Report Generator screen select Sales Ledger to display the first of two Sales Ledger Report Generator screens.

---

**Activity 37.1**          Naming a report

As you will see from the first Sales Ledger report generator screen the highlight is under the word NAME. This is where you enter the name of the report - this one will be called SALES. Type in:

> **SALES**

and press **RETURN** to complete the entry. Immediately, a prompt appears in the upper portion of the screen:

> **Do you want to    :    Run  Edit  Print  Delete**

At the moment you have no report to Run, Print or Delete. To create the report you will have to select Edit by typing **E**. The highlight now moves under the heading TITLE. Type in the title as:

> **Sales Ledger Report for August 1992**

When you complete this entry by pressing **RETURN** the screen display changes to the second Report Generator screen.

**Activity 37.2**   Viewing the second Report Generator screen

The details of the report's construction are to be entered into this second screen. Down the left hand side of the screen are the letters A, B, C, ... and there is a highlight on the letter A. Press **PgDn** a number of times and you will see that these letters range through A to Z and then a to z making 52 letters in all. The report will be created by listing variables against these letters thereby permitting up to 52 variables to form the report. To understand what is mean by a variable press the function key **F4** and a small window will be displayed in the right half of the screen. In this window you will see a list of variables - the first being Account Ref. These variables will form the headings of the report and are inserted into the report generator screen from this window. Press **PgDn** three times and you will see the complete list of variables that are available. Press **PgUp** three times to return the highlight to the top of the list of variables.

Press **ESC** to remove the window display and now press **PgUp** until the highlight is back on the letter A. Before you set about creating the report press **F1** and you will see a Help window displayed. The information in this screen is telling you the effects of the **F4** and **F3** function keys. Press **F1** again and the second Help screen gives you information concerning the labels Len, Sort, Brk, Tot and CD that are displayed across the top of the Report Generator screen. Do not worry if they do not make too much sense at the moment. By the time you have generated your first report their meanings will become crystal clear. Press **ESC** and the Help screen disappears.

**Activity 37.3**   Creating a report

Ensure that the highlight is on the letter A and press the **F4** function key. The variable window now appears with a highlight on the first variable Account Ref. Press **RETURN** and this variable name now appears alongside the letter A in the Report Generator screen - the number 6 under Len represents 6 characters, being the length of the variable.

The highlight in the variable window has now moved to the next variable - Account Name and the highlight in the report generator screen has moved down to the letter B. This is how variables are entered into the report.

Place the following variables in the report generator screen (you will have to move the highlight up and down the list of variables as they are not in the same order as the list required in the report):

**Account Name**
**Analysis Code**
**Balance**
**Nominal A/C**
**Amount Paid**
**Amount Due**
**Payment Date**

When these entries are complete press **ESC** to remove the variable window. You now realise that the Nominal Account variable is not required. You need to remove it so place the highlight over the letter E alongside the Nominal Account varaible and press **F4** to display the variable window. Press **PgDn** until you see at the bottom of the list the words Remove Field. Place the highlight over this and press **RETURN**. Immediately, the Nominal Account variable disappears and the following three variables move up a space to take its place.

The report definition is almost complete. We have yet to consider those legends Len, Sort, Brk, Tot and CD. We shall do that later - for now look at the numbers listed under Len. Len stands for Length and the numbers represent the maximum numbers of characters that can appear under each variable heading.

Now press **F3** and at the top of the screen you will see how the variable names will appear on the printed report. You cannot see them all so press **F10** a number of times and you will see the list move to the left. Press **F9** and the list moves back again. Press **F3** to remove the display.

---

**Activity 37.4**     Running a report

Ensure that the second Report Generator screen is on display without the variable window. Press **ESC** and the prompt:

**Do you want to     :     Save     Edit     Abandon**

re-appears. Select Save by typing **S** and the report definition will be saved to disk. When this is complete you are confronted with the first Report Generator screen. Press **RETURN** and a prompt appears at the top of the screen:

**Do you want to     :     Run     Edit     Print     Delete**

Select the default Run by pressing **RETURN**. You will then be confronted with a list of questions:

**Lower Account Reference   000000**       :   Press **RETURN**

**Upper Account Reference   ZZZZZZ**       :   Press **RETURN**

**Enter Date of Report**         **010892**       :   **310892**

**Print, File or View**           **P**           :   Press **RETURN**

The report is then sent to the printer.

Editing a report

From the printout of the report you will now appreciate the role of the variables. Each variable forms a heading to the report and the various values of the variables that apply are listed beneath each heading.

From the appearance of the report you will also appreciate that the information it conveys is rather muddled. Some of the variable values are repeated, they are not in any coherent order and there are numbers without totals. You will now see how to improve this state of affairs.

After the report was printed you found that the screen display returned to the first screen of the report generator with the SALES report visible. Press **RETURN** and at the prompt select Edit. The highlight moves to the Title. You do not wish to edit this so press **RETURN** to obtain the display of the second Report Generator screen. The highlight is on the letter A again. Press **RIGHT ARROW** and the flashing cursor moves to the space beneath Sort.

Now press **F1** again to reveal the Help display and then press **F1** to display the second Help screen. Read the description relating to Sort. You are going to want the Account Reference values to be listed in alphabetical order so you are going to want 1A to be entered against this field under Sort. Press **ESC** to remove the Help display and enter **1A** under Sort for the Account Reference variable. Press **RETURN** to complete your entry and the flashing cursor moves under Brk.

Read the Help information about Brk and then enter **L** in this space. There will be a line Break after each variable value. Move the highlight to the Balance variable and place a **Y** under Tot so that for each Account Reference the Balance Values will be totalled.

Your report is now complete. Press **ESC** and at the prompt select Save. When the report is Saved press **RETURN** and at the prompt select Run and when your new report is printed you will appreciate the effect of what you have just done.

On your new report you will see that the Analysis Code values are repeated unnecessarily. To avoid this re-edit the report and put a line break alongside Analysis Code.

When this Activity is complete press **ESC** twice to return to the Main Menu.

**Key words**            **Report Generator**

Task 38       **Departmental analysis**

**Objective**

To learn how to assign activities to Departments and how to create a Departmental report.

**Instructions**

From the Main Menu select Utilities to display the Utilities screen.

> **Departments**
> **VAT Code Changes**
> **Month End**
> **Year End**
> **Data File Utilities**
> **Backup Utilities**

---

**Activity 38.1**      Namimg Departments

From the Utilities screen select Departments to display the prompt:

> **Do you want to     :     View     Edit**

Select Edit by typing **E** and the Department screen will be displayed. For each Department you will have to enter a number and a name. At the prompt:

> **Department No.    :**

Enter the number **1** and opposite Department Name the legend:

> **UNUSED DEPARTMENT**

appears. Press **DELETE** until this disappears and type in the Department name:

> **Timber**

Press **RETURN** and the next department is awaiting naming. Name and number the following three Departments:

> **2   Scallops**
> **3   Oysters**
> **4   Scallops & Oysters**

Press **ESC** to complete the Department Editiing and you are returned to the Utilities screen. Press **ESC** and you are returned to the Main Menu.

| **Activity 38.2** | Creating a Departmental Analysis |
|---|---|

From the Main Menu select Report Generator and from the Report Generator screen select Management Reports. Into the first screen of the Management Reports report generator enter:

**NAME as DEPT**
**TITLE as Departmental Analysis**

In the second screen of the Report Generator place the following variables against A to G:

**Department No.**
**Department Name**
**Amount-Nett**
**Amount-Paid**
**Amount-Due**
**Type (Long)**
**Type (Short)**

Sort Department No. in alphabetical order (taken to also include numerical order); put a line Break after Department No., Department Name and Totals in the case of all three Amounts.

When you run this report and you are aked for Transaction Numbers and Dates, press **RETURN** to accept each default. From the printout you will see that all those transactions for which you entered a default department number as 0 are also listed. There is no way of avoiding this.

| **Key words** | **Utilities** |
|---|---|
| | **Department** |
| | **Departmental Analysis** |

Task 39      # The Nominal Ledger Monthly Accounts

**Objective**

To produce a Profit and Loss Report, a Balance Sheet, a Budget Report and to create the month-end files.

**Instructions**

From the Main Menu select the Nominal Ledger and from the Nominal Ledger screen select Nominal Account Structure to display the Nominal Account Structure screen:

> **Account Names**
> **Profit & Loss Format**
> **Balance Sheet Format**

---

**Activity 39.1**

Viewing the Profit and Loss Account format

From the Nominal Account Structure screen select Profit & Loss Format. The Profit and Loss Format screen displays six categories:

> **Sales**
> **Purchases**
> **Direct Expenses**
> **Overheads 1**
> **Overheads 2**
> **Overheads 3**

Select each one in turn and see which Nominal Ledger codes are assigned to which category. You will find that the default codes do not necessarily coincide with the codes you have been using. Edit the Profit & Loss Format as follows:

|  | **Low** | **High** |
|---|---|---|
| **Sales** | 1001 | 1001 |
| **Purchases** | 1001 | 1001 |
| **Direct Expenses** | | |
| **Overheads 1** | 7200 | 8204 |
| **Overheads 2** | 1103 | 1103 |
| **Overheads 3** | | |

When you are satisfied that your editing is complete press **ESC** to return to the Profit & Loss Format screen. Select another category and proceed until you have completed the editing of the entire report. From the Profit & Loss Format screen press **ESC** to return to the Nominal Account Structure screen.

---

**Activity 39.2**     Viewing the Balance Sheet format

From the Nominal Account Structure screen select Balance Sheet Format. The Balance
Format screen displays four categories:

| | | |
|---|---|---|
| **Fixed Assets** | 0020 | 0051 |
| **Current Assets** | | |
| **Liabilities** | | |
| **Financed By** | | |

Select each one in turn and see which Nominal Ledger codes are assigned to which
category. We shall accept the default format for the Balance Sheet so press **ESC** twice to
return to the Nominal Ledger screen.

---

**Activity 39.3**     Producing the P & L Report and the Balance Sheet

From the Nominal Ledger screen select Monthly Accounts to display the Monthly Accounts
screen:

**P & L and Balance Sheet**
**Budget Report**
**Create Month End Files**

From the Monthly Accounts screen select P & L and Balance Sheet. The screen then
displays the prompt:

**Press ESC to finish, press RETURN to continue**

Press **RETURN** and a small window appears on the screen to indicate that the system is
reading data to construct the two reports. Eventually, you are asked:

**Printer, File or View**

Type **P** for Printer and wait for the hard copy to be produced at the printer. When the
reports have been produced you will have been returned to the Monthly Accounts screen.
Press **ESC** to return to the Nominal Ledger screen.

**Profit & Loss Report**
This report considers the Nominal Account PRODUCT SALES and displays your profit
and loss under two headings, This Month and Year to Date.

**Balance Sheet**
The Balance sheet considers the Nominal Accounts FIXED ASSETS, CURRENT ASSETS,
CURRENT LIABILITIES and FINANCED BY to produce a report under the two headings of
This Month and Year to Date.

**Activity 39.4**     To produce a Budget report

From the Nominal Ledger Monthly Accounts screen select Budget Report. In response to the request to enter a month number - accept the default of 1. This is the first accounting month and does not mean January. Elect to have the report sent to the printer.
   The report produces a large amount of zeros because a budget has only been set against one account, namely the BAD DEBT WRITE OFF account.

---

**Activity 39.5**     Creating the Month End Files

From the Main Menu select the Nominal Ledger and from the Nominal Ledger screen select Monthly Account. From the Monthly Accounts screen select Create Month End Files. A message is displayed:

> **This Routine will make a copy of the files recording the current Nominal Ledger Trial Balance for use at the end of the next month to calculate month-to-date figures for the Monthly Reports. You should run this option once only at the end of each month after producing the Profit & Loss, Balance Sheet and Budget Reports for that month.**
>
> **Press ESC to finish, RETURN to continue**

As you already have the reports referred to press **RETURN** to continue. What happens next depends upon the disk system you are using.

**Hard Disk**
If you have a hard disk system then the Month End files are created without any further intervention by you.

**Floppy Drive**
If you have a Data File disk in an external floppy drive then you will be asked to place a blank, formatted disk into the external drive so that the Month End files can be saved to that disk. You will have to swap your current disk with the new disk a number of times until the porocess is complete.

When the Month End Files have been created and saved to disk you will be returned to the Main Menu.

| Key words | Profit and Loss Report |
|-----------|------------------------|
|           | Balance Sheet          |
|           | Budget Report          |
|           | Asset Valuation Report |
|           | Create month-end files |

Task 40

# The VAT analysis

**Objective**

To learn how to produce the various reports related to the end of the accounting month.

**Instructions**

At the end of each accounting month you will require detailed information concerning the viability of your company during the previous month. To this end you will print out a collection of month-end reports and the VAT Return. In addition, the ledgers are balanced and the start of month files are cleared ready for the commencement of the next month's accounting. Ensure that the Main Menu is being displayed.

---

**Activity 40.1**

Viewing the VAT code structure

Before looking at a VAT Return Analysis is is best if you look at the VAT code structure. From the Main Menu select Utilities and from the Utilities screen select VAT Code Changes.

The VAT Code Changes screen lists a matrix of numbers - most of them being zero. Down the left hand side of the matrix is a list of T's and across the top of the matrix are the numbers 0 to 9. Under the intersection of the first row and the column headed 1 you will see the number 17.5. This is the current VAT tax rate in operation - the tax rate with code T1 that you have been using throughout. Notice that T0 is 0 as you would expect.

Using this matrix array it is possible to enter different VAT rates ranging from ZERO RATED at T0 to UNRATED at T9. Not only that, but it is also posssible to enter a different set of VAT rates for use if, for instance, you were trading with another member state of the EEC.

When you are satisfied that you appreciate the structure of this screen press **ESC** twice to return to the Main Menu.

---

**Activity 40.2**

Producing the VAT Return Analysis

From the Main Menu select Nominal Ledger and from the Nominal Ledger screen select VAT Return Analysis. On the VAT Return Analysis screen accept the default for the Lower and Upper Transaction numbers, the Date ranges and send the report to the Printer. At the prompt Tax Code just press **RETURN** twice and after a moment or two the VAT Return Analysis is sent to the printer.

You will notice that the analysis is in four parts:

**Sales Tax Analysis**
**Purchase Tax Analysis**
**Nominal Tax Analysis**
**Tax Analysis Summary**

With the aid of this report you will be able to complete your VAT return to the Customs and Excise.

| Key words | **Profit and Loss format and report**<br>**Balance Sheet format and report**<br>**VAT Return analysis** |
| --- | --- |

# Task 41

# Clearing unwanted files

**Objective**

To learn how to clear unwanted files from the disk.

**Instructions**

At the end of each accounting month you will have filled up a significant amount of disk space with files that are no longer of any use. These consist of invoices, credit notes and sales and purchase orders that have been fully processed.

To reclaim space on the disk you will now erase them. Ensure that the Main Menu is on display.

---

**Activity 41.1**

Deleting Invoices

To ensure that you do not fill all the avilable disk space with unwanted information we can now delete all issued invoices. From the Main Menu select Sales Ledger and from the Sales Ledger screen select Invoice Production. From the Invoice Production screen select Delete Invoices. The system will then ask for the Lower and Upper invoice numbers. Press **RETURN** to accept the default in each case. The system will then scan through each invoice checking to see if it has been printed and posted. If it has then it will be deleted from the disk. When it arrives at the LEE invoice for the PART filled sales order you will see the warning message:

**Invoice No X**

**Warning! Invoice has not been posted**

or:

**Warning! Invoice has not been printed**

**Confirm deletion: No Yes**

Select No. When you have deleted all unwanted invoices press **ESC** twice to return to the Main Menu.

---

**Activity 41.2**

Deleting Sales and Purchase Orders

Just as all unwanted invoices can be deleted so can all despatched and cancelled sales orders.

From the Main Menu select Sales Order Processing and from the Sales Order Processing screen select Delete Orders. Press **RETURN** at the Lower and Upper Order Number request to accept the default. The system will then delete any despatched sales order.

All completed Purchase Orders are deleted in the same way via the Purchase Order Processing facility.

# Section E: The second month

Your second month sees a number of problems arise in your trading. You will learn how to make a contra entry, how to deal with a returned cheque and a subsequent bad debt. You will learn how to account for refunds to customers and refunds from suppliers, how to increase the value of your stock in line with inflation and how to cater for a change in the VAT rate.

The following table describes which of the Tasks in this Section are available in which component of the Sage Sterling Accounting system:

| Task | 42 | 43 | 44 | 45 | 46 | 47 | 48 | 49 | 50 | 51 |
|------|----|----|----|----|----|----|----|----|----|----|
| Bookkeeper | no | yes | no | no | no | no | no | no | yes | yes |
| Accountant | no | yes | yes | no | yes | yes | yes | yes | yes | yes |
| Accountant + | yes | yes | yes | yes | yes | yes | yes | yes | yes | yes |
| Financial Controller | yes | yes | yes | yes | yes | yes | yes | yes | yes | yes |

# Task 42

## Outstanding purchase and sale invoices

**Objective**

To learn how to obtain information from the system that will inform you of all outstanding invoices that either need to be paid to the company or need to be paid by the company.

**Instructions**

At the commencement of a month's trading you will need to know how much you are owed and by whom. You will also need to know how much and to whom you yourself owe money. This information can be gleaned via the Report Generator that is accessed from the Main Menu.

Ensure that the Main Menu is being displayed and select Report Generator.

---

**Activity 42.1**

Outstanding sales payments

From the Report Generator screen select Sales Ledger to display the first Sales Ledger Report Generator screen. The cursor is currently beneath the heading NAME. Enter the name of an existing report - SALES - here and the details of the SALES report will appear.
Press **RETURN** and a prompt appears at the top of the screen:

**Do you want to    :    Run    Save    Edit    Delete**

Select Run and as in an earlier Task you produce a report of all outstanding debts owed to you by your customers. When the report has been produced you will be returned to the first Sales Ledger Report Generator screen. Press **ESC** to return to the Report Generator screen.

---

**Activity 42.2**

Outstanding purchase payments

To repeat the previous Activity for the Purchase Ledger and thereby find out to whom you owe money and how much we must first create a report.
From the Report Generator screen select Purchase Ledger and create a report called PURCH with title:

**Outstanding Purchases (August/September)**

The variable to include in this report are:

**Account Ref.**
**Account Name**
**Balance-30 Day**
**Details**
**Amount-Gross**
**Payment Date**

**Amount-Due**

When you have completed the definition of content and layout of your report Save it to disk and then Run it, producing a printout for future reference.

---

**Activity 42.3**

Viewing outstanding payments via the Transaction History

An alternative method of obtaining information regarding outstanding invoices is to consult the Transaction Histories of both the Sales and the Puchase Ledgers. When you do this you will find that certain transactions have a star against the Value. The star indicates that the invoice is outstanding.

In the Sales Ledger the outstanding invoices are:

| | |
|---|---|
| **JONES** | **2095.54** |
| **LEE** | **1245.00** |
| **OACH** | **4842.64** |
| **SMITH** | **1500.00** |

and in the Purchase Ledger they are:

| | |
|---|---|
| **ABC** | **540.00** |
| **HISEA** | **3254.79** |
| **WOOD** | **1037.11** |

---

**Key words**      **Outstanding sale payments**
**Outstanding purchase payments**

Task 43　　　　**Entering further receipts and payments**

**Objective**　　To review the processes involved in entering and posting receipts and payments.

**Instructions**　　In the light of the previous two reports that you produced in Task 42 you have written to those customers who owe you money and requested immediate payment. All but one have sent you what they owe and have been paid into the bank. In addition you have paid your suppliers the amounts that you owe them. These transactions must now be entered into the ledgers.

---

**Activity 43.1**　　Sales payments

Post the following Sales Recipts into the Sales Ledger:

| | |
|---|---|
| **JONES** | **2095.54** |
| **LEE** | **1245.00** |
| **OACH** | **4842.64** |

Enter the date as 250992. Select Payment Method as Automatic and you will see the word FULL on each transaction. Only the first transaction is highlighted but when you press **ESC** and post the receipts, all three will be posted.

---

**Activity 43.2**　　Purchase payments

Post the following Purchase Payments into the Purchase Ledger.

| | |
|---|---|
| **ABC** | **540.00** |
| **HISEA** | **3254.79** |
| **WOOD** | **1037.11** |

Enter the date as 250992. Select Payment Method as Automatic and you will see the word FULL on each transaction. Only the first transaction is highlighted but when your press **ESC** and post the payments then all three will be posted.

---

**Activity 43.3**　　Cash flow

All your customer's, bar one, have paid you in full and you have paid all your suppliers. You now wish to look at your bank account to see the state of affairs there. From the Main

Menu select Nominal Ledger and from the Nominal Ledger screen select Control Account History. From the Control Account History screen select Bank Accounts. Accept all the defaults on the Bank Accounts screen to give you a display of every bank transaction that has been made. Press **RETURN** until you see the end of the list and at the bottom of the screen your bank balance is displayed. A debit of £6978.03. Your cash flow is in order, you have money in the bank.

**Key words**    **Bank Receipts**
**Bank Payments**

# Task 44

## Contra entries

**Objectives:**

To learn how to enter a Contra Entry.

**Instructions**

Occasionally one of your company suppliers is also a customer in which case a sale can be off-set by a corresponding purchase. In this instance the company has purchased its first month's supply of diesel for the van from the local garage. In the second month the garage owner has asked for a supply of timber and you have agreed to off-set the sale by supplying timber to the same value as the diesel fuel purchsed. In this way no cash is transferred between the company and the garage but because the stock level of timber has been reduced the two transactions must be recorded in the accounting system. This is done by posting a Contra Entry.

---

**Activity 44.1**

Posting the garage purchase order for diesel fuel

The purchase order details for the first month's deisel fuel arrivod during the second month. The details are:

**Bayview Garage**
**Isle of Erin**

**31 Aug 92**

**Invoice: 334**

**To diesel fuel for August:**           **125.35**

VAT   :     **21.94**

--------

TOTAL  :   **147.29**

Set up a supplier account using the Account Reference BAYP for the garage and enter the Purchase Invoice using Batched Data Entry from the Purchase Ledger screen and Nominal Account code 7300 for FUEL & OIL EXPENSES

---

**Activity 44.2**

Posting the sale order for timber to the garage

The sale order details for the delivery of timber to the Bayview Garage during the second month are:

**To:**

**Bayview Garage**
**Ise of Erin**

**5 Sep 92**

**Invoice: 12**

**To timber supply:**

**5 tonnes at £25.07 per tonne:**                                    125.35

                                                         VAT   :   21.94
                                                                   ———
                                                      TOTAL   :   147.29

Set up a customer account using the Account Reference BAYS for the garage and enter
the Sale order using Batched Data Entry from the Sales Ledger screen, remembering that the
Tax Code is T0, the Nominal Code is 1001 and the Department number is 1. When you
have done this produce a Sales Invoice using the Invoicing From Stock facility. Notice the
different Account References BAYP and BAYS for the Sales and Purchase Ledgers. This is
not necessary but it does help to separate sales and purchases when a customer is also a
supplier.

---

| Activity 44.3 | Posting the Contra Entry |
|---|---|

From the Main Menu select the Sales Ledger and from the Sales Ledger screen select
Contra Entries. Enter the following into the Contra Entry screen:

**Bank A/C**      :   **1200**
**Sales A/C**     :   **BAYS**
**Purchase A/C**  :   **BAYP**

All the outstanding Sales and Purchase Invoices are then displayed. In this case there is
just one of each.

Select the Sales Invoice by highlighting it and pressing **RETURN** and a Y appears
under P. The same procedure is used to select the Purchase Invoice. When you are
satisfied that the entries are correct press **ESC** to complete the entry and select Post from
the displayed prompt to post the contra entry to the ledgers.

When the posting is complete press **ESC** to return to the Sales Ledger screen.

---

| **Key words** | **Contra entries** |
|---|---|
| | **Sales and Purchase Invoices** |

Task 45    **Credit notes**

**Objective**    To learn how to issue a credit note.

**Instructions**    Of the oysters delivered to F Smith some 250 were dead on arrival. The company has always undertaken to supply live oysters so you must stand the loss.

---

**Activity 45.1**    Issuing a credit note

From the Main Menu select the Sales Ledger and from the Sales Ledger screen select Invoice Production. From the Invoice Production screen select Credit Note Production and enter the following details into the Credit Note Production screen:

| | | | |
|---|---|---|---|
| **Credit Note No.** | : | **1** | This is the default value |
| **Date** | : | **150992** | |
| **Sales Ref.** | : | **SMITH** | |

The procedure for creating the credit note is the same as that for producing an invoice from stock.

As the Tax Code for the original transaction was T0 so is the tax code for this credit note. The Tax Amount is, therefore, zero. When you have completed the posting of this credit note select Update Ledgers from the Stock Control screen.

Finally, display the Sales Ledger Transaction History for SMITH and you will see that he still owes £1500.00.

---

**Activity 45.2**    Issuing a statement and credit note

In Task 23 you learnt how to issue statements to customers. Issue a new statement to F Smith and Son Ltd and there you will see the credit displayed.

In Task 20 you learnt how to print an invoice. Repeat this procedure and you will produce the printed credit note.

---

**Key words**    **Credit note**

Task 46 | **Returned cheques**

**Objective**

To learn how to cancel a posted bank receipt.

**Instructions**

Occasionally the company will receive a cheque in payment for a Sales Invoice for which the customer does not have sufficient fund to meet. In such a case the cheque is returned to drawer which is your company. If you have already posted this payment through your accounts you will now have to cancel the posting. However, when you do so you will not cancel the tax liability - your company is still liable for the tax that was displayed on the original Sales Invoice. As a consequence, the next time you issue an invoice to cover the next attempt by your customer to pay debt, the tax code T9 must be used.

---

**Activity 46.1**

Posting a bank receipt

F Smith and Son have responded to the last statement that you sent them and have sent a cheque to the value of £1500.00 by return post. This you immediately paid into the bank.
    Post the details of the sales receipt.

---

**Activity 46.2**

Cancelling the cheque

One week after you had paid Smith's cheque into the bank it is returned to you as 're-turned to drawer'. You contact Smith by phone and he promises to send another cheque. Meanwhile you must abstract the posted cheque from your accounts.
    From the Main Menu select the Sales Ledger and from the Sales Ledger screen select Refunds. From the Refunds screen select Cancel Cheque and into the Cancel cheque screen enter the following details:

**A/C Ref.   :   SMITH**

The posted cheque appears on the screen, the details highlighted. Press **RETURN** to cancel this cheque and the Status is annotated as BOUNCED. Press **ESC** and select Post from the prompt to post this cancellation to the ledgers.
    Press **ESC** twice to return to the Sales Ledger screen. Select Transaction History and view the SMITH account. As you will see he still owes £1500.00.

---

**Key words**

**Returned cheques**
**Cancel Cheque**

Task 47    **Bad Debt Write-Off**

**Objective**    To learn how to write-off a bad debt from the accounts.

**Instructions**    F Smith and Son Ltd have failed to send the replacement cheque to cover the one that
bounced. After repeated attempts to contact the customer you receive the news that they
have ceased trading and bankruptcy procedings are pending. At a creditor's meeting you
find out that after all secured debts are covered there will be no money left to cover
unsecured debtors such as yourself. As a consequence the outstanding amount owed by F
Smith must be written off the books as a bed debt.

---

**Activity 47.1**    Writing off a bad debt

From the Sales Ledger screens select Bad Debt Write Off to display the Bad Debt Write
Off screen:

**Write Off Account**
**Write Off Small Values**
**Write Off Transactions**

From the Bad Debt Write Off screen select Write Off Account. At the prompt enter the
Account Reference SMITH and press **RETURN** . The screen then displays all outstanding
amounts owing by this account. At the prompt select Yes by pressing **RIGHT ARROW**
to highlight the Yes and then press **RETURN** to write off the account. The system will then
automatically write off the account.
    When the account has been written off a Credit note will exists on the system to the
value of the amount written off. Also note that the tax liability is not changed - that will
have to be a matter between your company and the Customs and Excise.
    Press **ESC** three times to return to the Main Menu.

---

**Activity 47.2**    Viewing the BUDGET WRITE OFF Account

From the Main Menu select the Nominal Ledger and from the Nominal Ledger screen
select Transaction History. Into the Transaction History screen enter the Lower and Upper
Account References as 8100 and opt for the Display. You will then see the Bad Debt
Write Off transaction displayed.

---

**Key words**    **Bad Debt Write Off**

## Task 48

# Refunding a customer

**Objective**

To learn how to account for a refund to a customer.

**Instructions**

Your delivery to JONES on 24th August last of 10 dozen scallops was found unfit for use some time after they had taken delivery. Your customer reported this fact to you and you agreed to reimburse him. As he was a cash customer he paid COD and he did not want a credit note. Instead he wanted a refund of all the money he had paid on receipt of the goods. From the Main Menu select the Sales Ledger to display the Sales Ledger screen.

---

**Activity 48.1**

Refund invoice

From the Sales Ledger screen select Refunds to display the Refunds screen:

**Cancel Cheque**
**Refund Invoice**

Select Refund Invoice and into the Refund Invoice screen enter the Account Reference as JONES.
Three transactions are displayed:

| | |
|---|---|
| **Scallops** | **1321.54** |
| **Scallops** | **684.00** |
| **Scallops** | **90.00** |

Move the highlight to the last transaction and press **RETURN** . The transaction is then marked as REFUNDED under Status. Press **ESC** and from the prompt select Post to post the transaction to the ledgers.

---

**Activity 48.2**

Checking the posting

Display the Nominal Ledger screen and select Control Account History. From the Control Account History select Bank Accounts and there you will find, at the end of the list of transactions, the postings for both SMITH and JONES.

---

**Key words**        **Customer Refunds**

# Task 49

## Supplier refunds

**Objective**

To learn how to account for a refund from a supplier.

**Instructions**

Your delivery from HISEA on 22nd August last of 50 dozen scallops was found unfit for use some time after you had taken delivery. You reported this fact to your supplier and you agreed that he would reimburse you. As you are a cash customer you paid COD and you did not want a credit note. Instead you wanted a refund of all the money you had paid on receipt of the goods. From the Main Menu select the Purchase Ledger to display the Purchase Ledger screen

---

**Activity 49.1**

Refund invoice

From the Purchase Ledger screen select Refunds to display the Refunds screen:

**Cancel Cheque**
**Refund Invoice**

Select Refund Invoice and into the Refund Invoice screen enter the Account Reference as HISEA.

Four transactions are displayed. Move the highlight to the last transaction and press **RETURN** . The transaction is then marked as REFUNDED under Status. Press **ESC** and from the prompt select Post to post the transaction to the ledgers.

Press **ESC** three times to return to the Main Menu.

---

**Activity 49.2**

Checking the posting

From the Main Menu select Nominal Ledger to display the Nominal Ledger screen and select Control Account History. From the Control Account History select Bank Accounts and there you will find, at the end of the list of transactions, the posting for HISEA.

---

**Key words**     **Supplier Refunds**

Task 50                    **Petty cash transactions**

**Objective**              To learn how to account for petty cash transactions.

**Instructions**           You are taking a trip to the mainland and you need cash to purchase stationery for the
                           company. This will mean a withdrawal into Petty Cash and such withdrawals are recorded
                           in the system via a Journal Entry.
                                From the Main Menu select the Nominal Ledger and from the Nominal Ledger screen
                           select Journal Entries.

---

**Activity 50.1**          Transferring money to petty cash

                           Date the transaction as 150992 and Debit the Petty Cash Account (account reference
                           1230) with 100.00. Credit the withdrawal to the bank current account with account
                           reference 1200.
                                Press **ESC** and select Post from the prompt to post the transaction to the Nominal
                           Ledger.

---

**Activity 50.2**          Processing cash transactions

                           You have purchased office stationery to the value of £68.50 plus VAT of £11.99 and you
                           now wish to record this transaction.
                                From the Nominal Ledger screen select Petty Cash Transactions and from the Petty
                           Cash Transactions screen select Cash Payment. Enter the details of the purchase receipt,
                           date 16th September into the Cash Payment screen using Nominal Code 5000 for
                           MATERIALS PURCHASES.

---

**Activity 50.3**          Transferring money from petty cash to the bank

                           You have £20.51 change left from the original £100 that you withdrew to purchase
                           stationery.  You have put this back into the bank and now you wish to record that transac-
                           tion. Again it will be a Journal Entry.
                                Date the transaction as 170992 and Credit the Petty Cash Account (account reference
                           1230) with 20.51. Debit the payment into the bank current account with account  refer-
                           ence 1200.
                                Press **ESC** and select Post from the prompt to post the transaction to the Nominal
                           Ledger.

| Key words | Petty cash transactions |
|---|---|
| | Journal Entries |

# Global changes

**Objective**

To learn how to make global changes to the accounting system.

**Instructions**

From your experience you find that the optional 5% discount that you have available is sometimes too low. You wish to increase it to 10% yet still retain the option of only giving 5%

From the Main Menu select Utilities and from the Utilities screen select Data File Utilities to display the Data File Utilities screen:

**Control Accounts**
**Global Changes**
**Posting Error Corrections**
**Data-File Changes**
**Data Verification**
**File-Import**

From the Data File Utilities screen select Global Changes to display the Global Changes screen:

**Ledger Files**
**Stock Files**

---

**Activity 51.1**

To make a global change to discounts

From the Global Changes screen select Stock Files to display the following:

**Sales Price**
**Purchase Price**
**Re-Order Level**
**Re-Order Quantity**
**Discount A**
**Discount B**
**Discount C**

Select Discount A and the following display appears:

**Add Amount**
**Subtract Amount**
**Multiply By**
**Divide By**
**Increase By %**
**Decrease By %**
**Give Figure**

Select Add Amount and the following prompt appears:

**Amount to Change to  :    0.00**

Type in **5** and press **RETURN**. Accept the three default options that appear relating to Categories or Stock Codes and a warning will be issued.

**This program will now Add 5.00 to the Discount A
WARNING! The following chnages are NOT reversible**

**Do you want to     :    Finish    Continue**

Select Continue to effect the global change.

Check the Stock Details from the Stock Control screen and you will see that all the Discount A% figures now read 10.00.

---

**Activity 51.2**

To change Dicount B from 0% to 5%

Repeat the previous Activity and increase the Discount B to 5%.

---

**Activity 51.3**

To make a global change to the ledger files

From the Global Changes screen select Ledger Files to display the Ledger Files screen:

**Sales Turnover**
**Sales Credit Limit**
**Purchase Turnover**
**Purchase Credit Limit**
**Nominal Budgets**

Select Nominal Budgets and increase the BAD DEBT WRITE OFF account (Account Reference 8100) provision by 10%.

When you have completed this view the result by selecting Account Names from the Nominal Account Structure selection from the Nominal Ledger screen. You will see that the yearly budget is now set at £3300 with each monthly figure at £275.

Press **ESC** three times to return to the Main Menu and select Quit to leave the system.

Key words          Global changes
                  Stock files
                  Ledger files